PROFILE OF INDIAN WOMAN MANAGERS

A Cascading Journey from Myths to Reality

PROF. INDIRA J PARIKH
MAHRUKH F. ENGINEER

INDIA · SINGAPORE · MALAYSIA

Notion Press

No. 8, 3rd Cross Street,
CIT Colony, Mylapore,
Chennai, Tamil Nadu – 600 004

First Published by Notion Press 2020
Copyright © Prof. Indira J Parikh, Mahrukh F. Engineer 2020
All Rights Reserved.

ISBN 978-1-64983-818-6

DEDICATION

This book is a joint book written by Mahrukh and Indira Parikh. This book ought to have been finished a long time ago at least 15 years back, but various situations and events did not make it possible to work on it. In the meantime, Mahrukh Engineer passed away, and I felt compelled from within to complete this book so much that I decided I would complete the book.

The book began because Mahrukh wanted to write something with me. Mahrukh wandered into my office one day in the afternoon at the Indian Institute of Management Ahmedabad. She said now I have found the person I want to work with and learn from. I asked what she meant by that statement. She said I am at that stage of my life where I want to do something meaningful and relevant. She said I want to so do something which I would be remembered by.

I was to present a paper in women, so I said let it be a joint paper. You work on that. And she did. When it was time to present the paper, which was circulated as the working paper, it was on my table. I then saw that Mahrukh had printed the paper in my name alone. So far, I have been doing work alone. I stopped in the middle and said I have to apologize. I apologized to Mahrukh in public and said she is the co-author, and a lot of credit goes to her.

We then thought of writing this as a book. She worked hard on this book. Went to interview many women from across the country. And some women like Anu Aga made a tremendous impact on her. She came one day and said I am so impressed with Anu that I will have a daughter and then name her Anu. And she did have a daughter and name, dear Anaya.

The book got delayed by a decade as I went to Pune to start FLAME. And we spoke in between to complete the book. Then one day, her phone calls stopped coming. I wondered what happened. And then I heard that she was no more. It was a shock of sorrow and sadness as she was a dear friend. And she was young. I remembered vividly one incident and experience.

This book should have completed a since an all decades earlier, and thus decade much has changed and not changes. To remember Mahrukh and her kindness. Let me share a beautiful story. My husband was detected with cancer. And we had to give him chicken soup. My household being vegetarian, I was wondering what to do. I called Mahrukh and asked if she knew any family who could provide daily some chicken soup. She said she would provide for the next three months before left for Pune she sends with her driver chicken soup. The box was beautifully packed that anyone could be tempted to open the box. From my side, I would fill the same box with Gujarathi dishes like the Khakhra, bhakhri, and muthiya. Mahrukh had four relatives all above eighty and ninety and they loved the bhakhris we enjoyed the exchange of food on daily basis.

I am please that finally the book has seen the light of day. I hope somewhere where've Mahrukh is she would be pleased that her dream to wrote and publish a book has come true. She has done tons of effort in interviewing women and excitedly sharing her learning.

Indira Parikh

Contents

Acknowledgment

This book is about women who have made departures, taken a path that was not meant for them. They reached their destination against all odds and lack of support systems. They received support from most unusual people. These are stories of heroism, pain and sorrow and moments of immense experience of freedom and achievements. Reaching their destinations, demanded immense self discipline, patience, acceptance of their self worth, self esteem and trust in their choices. They have accepted the consequences of their choices and decisions. They climbed the uncharted terrain of their lives, the loneliness of wilderness and step by step they reached each milestone and created new landmark.

In this book, there is only one story of Anu Aga. However, many women participated in the study. For example, a program in IIMA of senior women managers of ONGC, Indian Oil and several other private and public sector organization. Anu Aga gave detailed information and hours and hours of time to Mahrukh sharing of her life history. Her story is like many other stories of successful men's wives. These were the talented women who had no purpose or meaning of life but being a wife of big man. They did kitty parties, played Mahjong and self frustrated that they were not utilizing their potential or actualizing their aspirations of doing something meaningful. Then one day came a life defining moments when Anu Aga joined her husband's organization in HR as a subordinate junior employee to Mr. Prasad and learnt all about HR. With the tragic moment of her husband loss, she was ready to take the charge of the organization and did the best she could which was very good. Similar are all the stories of many women who in crises of loss taken up the helm of the institutions and run it successfully.

Much of the credit also goes to Dr Bharti Venkatesh who took upon herself to revive this project and said ma'am we need to complete this book. She knew Mahrukh a little bit when Mahrukh joined me in IIM to work at that time Bharti was my Research Associate.

At this point in time, I would like to thank the Indian Institute of Management, Ahmedabad (IIM-A), for providing me time while I was there to work on this book. I need to thank others who have helped in preparing this book. My secretary in IIM Ahmedabad Mrs. Vijaya Priya, who has helped quite extensively in preparing the scheduling of the meetings and typing and retyping the manuscript. I would also like to thank FLAME that gave me time to pick up this project for a little while before I gave it up and waited until now to complete this project. I would also like to thank my Flame staff, especially Mrs. Pragati Chopra Shah, Sonali Joshi, and Rajashree Chaudhary.

Thanks to my personal family, especially my husband Jitendra Parikh and my son Sushrut Parikh who is a close friend of Mahrukh's husband. I would also like to thank my staff at home, who made it possible for me to work in extended hours without complaints. Most importantly, Ananda, who has been in my family for 50 years, and he made sure that everything at home run smoothly so that I can give my time to work.

Prof. Indira J Parikh

Women in Management - A Movement from the Fifties to the New Millennium

Introduction

Women's roles and so also men's roles exist in the context of society and culture, which allocates and defines roles for both. Society and culture provide myths and epics depicting the journey of a hero as he unfolds his life to seek the answers to the questions of who am I and what is the purpose of life. However, there are no epics or myths where women take a journey and an adventure to unfold their lives to discover who they are. Their stories and their lives are always around relationships, search for meanings in relationships and sacrifice or investment in relationships. The women have lived contained within a narrow space, shrunken roles, and frozen initiatives. After centuries of agrarian living technological revolution and industrialization opened the minds of women shattering the myths that they need to walk a few steps behind. Women journeyed into educational fields and then organizations and work outside the home. This journey was undertaken in four stages over five decades. In this time, women have found answers to questions about their identity. It is now time for all womankind it is their role to build a new heritage, new role models and give shape to the destiny of the girl child of tomorrow and in the centuries to come.

Women carry a cultural heritage of five thousand years. The social structures and role processes which these women carry also belong to the traditional agrarian society, which is two thousand five hundred years old. The Indian women for long have been seeped in cultural lore of idealism and faith shackled within the context of involuntary conformity to social structures and roles, and marginalised vis-a-vis the males of the family.

After a hundred years of industrialisation and over fifty years of freedom, Indian women at the workplace are realising their dreams and finding their feet. Education opened doors for a lot of women who dared to dream, and to weave a fabric of life within which they could live their dreams and achieve their ambitions. The journey which many women took in this century began with the freedom movement and recently crossed the threshold of the new millennium. Women learnt to juggle multiple expectations and demands of the system at home and at the workplace. They remained rooted in their dreams of freedom, and their desire for self-fulfilment. Women in management are finally coming of age. The transformation of the Indian woman from an enigmatic figure covered in metres of fabric, to today's educated, successful and accomplished professional has not been without great personal sacrifices. This image is as real and alive as the arduous path she has travelled to arrive at her current destination. These are women who have broken shackles thousands of years old, who have walked a previously non traversed path, who have had the courage to make new beginnings and pay the price for the choices they have made.

Concept of Life Space

Concept of Life space is linked with experience of sensations. When a child is born as he comes out of the mother's womb the child experiences the mother's body and its experience of entering this world. The child experiences the deeply buried emotions of the mother and his/ her own emotions and feelings as to how it is deeply absorbed in the body. If you believe in many births then the concept goes deeper into what the child has lived through many lives are experienced within is with the child in the body of the child and the emotions of the child.

As the child enters this world the child's first experience is the contact with a set of people. Here is where the coding begins of life roles. It is a simultaneous process of being born and encountering people who receive him with acceptance or rejection or indifference. The child's experience of space and life roles is intertwined right from the moment of birth.

Transformation is an inevitable process. All living organisms transform themselves. Human beings know that they are transforming and experience the process of transformation. They articulate it through words, give meanings to it and to some extent give shape and direction to it.

Women are creations of human endeavor and they continue to evolve and acquire their own identity. Women's identity is shaped by multiple factors such as history of organization, philosophy of work, leadership, people and organization structure, tasks, goals and objectives. Moreover, this identity is crystallized through the dynamic interplay amongst these multiple factors. This identity unfolds and transforms through both internal and external energy of a women. The internal and external energy become the drivers of change. These are:

1. Internal environment i.e., drivers of change within the self
2. External environment i.e., drivers of change outside of the self

The interplay of these drivers of change gives shape to the identity of women. The drivers of change either cachet to the energy available within self or they become captive or frozen and immobilize themselves. Energy is of three kinds:

1. Captive Energy

2. Frozen Energy
3. Free Energy

These three energies determine the nature and direction of transformations, which occur or do not occur within the self. The sources of these three energies are in turn held by different constituencies at the:

1. Life Space
2. Social Space and
3. Work Space

Each of the above three constituencies may bring one or more of these energies into play which would impact an individual in different ways. Figure 1 presents the relationship between the three kinds of energy and the three levels of constituencies.

Figure 1

Energy and their Constituencies

	Captive (C)	Frozen (Fr)	Free (Fe)
Life Space (LS)	1	2	3
Social Space (SS)	4	5	6
Work Space (WS)	7	8	9

Let us look at the intensity of this energy, nature of the energy and the constituents that bring this energy in a dynamic relationship. The interplay of the various relationships between the nine boxes then impacts the self and its transformation. If the free energy is not utilized then the self does not grow. The self becomes captive or frozen to the constituencies and at some point of time creates immense dysfunctionalities within the self.

Let us now understand the concept of these three energy

1. **The Captive Energy:** Captive energy is that energy which once was free energy available within the individual. The individual was alive, movement oriented, directional and vibrant.

2. **The Frozen Energy**: The Frozen energy is that energy which reflects the state of relationships amongst the role holders.

3. **The Free Energy**: The Free energy is that energy which is with each individual, collective and the organization.

Figure 2
Interpretation of Energy and their Constituencies

	Captive	Frozen	Free
Life Space	They are role-bound, work within limited and narrow spaces, self righteous and idealistic	They are sensitive and touchy. They got tendencies of blaming others. They hold silent evaluation and are judgemental	Women in this zone are creative, intelligent, spontaneous, enthusiastic and energetic
Social Space	They are little hesitant and expect conformity and compliance to social norms. They blame society system	They tend to be comparative with others. They are competitive however, tend to put blame on individual rather than on themselves	They are responsive, sensitive, caring, nurturing and affirmed people
Work Space	They tend to wait for instruction. They blame other people for not completing the task. They are hesitant in taking the responsibility and do not take any accountability too	They are evaluative and judgmental in their thought process. They are highly critical of the people. They usually behave 'my way or high way' with other people. They carry lot of anger and self pity	They are assertive, and take responsibilities. They tend to take initiative and are action oriented. They meet deadline and do take charge of people and the system

The interplay and the nature and quality of the three forms of energy: – captive, frozen and free with the three constituencies: – the life space, the social space and the work space that the transformation occurs or does not occur of the individual, the collective and the organization. Whether the energy generated will dissipate or enhance is dependent once again on several factors.

Experiential Reality of Fantasy

This experience of Life space is also determined by the order of birth of the child. If the child is first born the child experiences larger space as all the space available to the child belongs to the first child as there is no other sibling to share the space. When the second child is born the space of the first child as well as the relatedness of the first child with all the adults is shared. If the experience and emotions of the first child at the time of birth is positive then the entry of the second child does not create any trauma and the first child is open to sharing the space with the new arrival. The second child for some time is the younger child. So gets the attention and the space from others. This also depends upon whether the first child is a girl child and the second child is a boy child. *If both the children are girl children and the family is obsessed with having a boy child the relatedness of the girl children will have a quality of inner uneasiness if they emotions are expressed vocally. Even if these are not voiced but the hankering of a male child is obvious the girl children will experience the hesitation to claim freely the space which belongs to them.* If then the third child is a male child he will get the maximum space in terms of relatedness and affection and some of the privileges which is said to for the youngest child. The human sensitivities are so sharp that no matter how and how much you hide the logical behaviour the deeper emotional expression in behaviour like tonality and the body posture impact the experience of emotional space, the nature of relatedness in the space and actual behaviour patterns.

Having said this now there are three children. The patterns of claiming the space of the eldest, the youngest and the middle child starts to superimpose on the experience of space. There are distinct patterns of behaviour in experiencing the space of the first born, the last born and the Middle child. All other children become one of many and they reflect different patterns of experiencing space.

Myths of Women Manager

India is a country where simultaneously juxtaposition of the ancient and the new, the traditional and the modern, the agrarian and the technological, the rural and the urban and the concept of east and the west coexist. The living reality of these juxtapositions is experienced in all spheres of life from be it women living in purdah to women wearing a business suit working in corporate offices taking international business decisions or men carrying loads on their back, tilling the soil to flying planes and designing state of the art technology. This transition both social and technological pushes women and men across the country to take new roles and to walk on a new path leading to an entirely new world, where there are three F's: Freedom, Fame and Fortune.

Last century has witnessed Indian women in a new persona. Apart from being daughters, wives and mothers, they entered into educational institutions and equipped themselves to take roles in the health sector and to become nurses and teachers. Then came the freedom movement and Indian women joined in the freedom struggle. When the time came for building the nation, women joined the educational institutions and finally entered into the fields of management in formal and industrial organizations. This spiral of women's history suggests that wherever the women have entered they have carved a niche for themselves. However, the acknowledgement and acceptance of this transition and transformation of women's role is a slow process. A large number of women, larger number of men and even larger portion of the society take a much longer time to acknowledge and accept the reality of women's capabilities and competencies. As the critical mass of women enters the new and diverse occupations the image of women will undergo change.

Across time women have walked the path of traditions. However, in walking these paths, they have made slow but steady departures. As and when the opportunities have come their way and as and when there are challenges thrown their way women, men and organizations have believed that women will not respond. Many women have surprised the world by taking those challenges and working against the odds. In times of crises and in times of immense emotional stress women have risen to the call to take charge of their families, home and destined to give shape to it and move forward.

Entering the organizations has been a formidable challenge. Moving from infrastructural roles of the sixties and rising to managerial roles and responsibilities which is almost a Herculean task, and rising into senior management position is an uphill struggle. For women to occupy the position of CEO's in the present scenario, which was a rarity and almost impossibility, today is a reality.

In this movement, let us take a look at the supportive and inhibitive forces, which has either facilitated or retarded women's growth:

External Environment

The external environment has created the universalization of education and the government has formulated policies to encourage the girl child for higher education. The educational institutions facilitated women to discover their competencies and achieve and succeed.

The external environment provides women the awareness and opportunities of career and occupation. Men simultaneously compete for these opportunities. In a fair for all arenas of job markets, women bring to the organization their education, their achievements and competence their determination and resilience. With this they also bring their doubts, emotional vulnerabilities and fragilities, which become the hallmark for women. Caught between competence and doubts, achievements and roadblocks of guilt and success and anxieties, women carry a unique juxtaposition of determination and ambivalence about breaking new paths and taking new roles.

Internal Environment

The internal environment of women consists of parental home and their own home, the society, neighbourhood and community as well as the internal dynamics of the work place.

Having entered the organization and having successfully competed with the male world, women encounter the labels of preferred treatment, having a godfather or using feminity as a means of entry. Having entered the organization in managerial positions with responsibility and authority, there are allegations of women entering the position through quota system and not merit. Women respond to these with some defiance, some defensiveness and some self-protection only to be labelled as insecure, unprofessional. By and large, the women are undervalued by the system. If her capabilities and competencies are accepted, respected and translated into operational roles, she creates anxieties, hostilities and aggression in others.

Similarly, in the home setting women are propelled to be educated, pulled to stay at home, pushed to take jobs to enhance the quality of life and condemned and accused for not playing their social roles. At another level, there is recognition of their achievements, supported to excel and encouraged to be professionals.

Women themselves accept that they have other meanings in life besides only the social roles and they have an internal evocation to enlarge their life space through commitment to growth.

Put together, the external and internal environment create opportunities and challenges as well as roadblocks to growth. These are present in varied intensities and it is up to the women to carve out a road map and niche for themselves.

Facilitating Processes and Support System

Now let us look at her social, personal and familial environment.

The family and parents educate the women and open up a new path of occupation and a world of work for women. The women aspire for the future of a job and a career eventually to grow into a professional.

Once she completes her education often excelling and proving her competence, marriage is around the corner. She marries and often than not compromises or marginalizes her career. If she does not, then automatically, it is assumed both by her personal family, the husband and his family that she is compromising marriage and her multiple social roles viz. that of a mother.

Women today share the workspace with men in almost all functions and areas. But women in top management positions are still a rare species. Globally, according to the Fortune 500 companies, less than 4% of the women are in the upper most ranks of CEO and less than 3% of the women are top corporate role holders in India. We may be able to find a handful of companies headed by women or women at the helm of strategic business units.

Formal organizations have structures, which are dominantly male focused. Similarly, management has traditionally implied maleness and thus has often carried with it particular managerial and leadership qualities. These qualities are what woman lack. The model of the successful manager has historically been a masculine one and the male managerial perspective is far more operative. As women have entered the formal work organization a decade later than men, and with social, cultural, and familial stereotypes it has taken women much longer to be in senior management positions and taking leadership roles. It is within this 'discrimination' and masculine paradigms that women learn to become managers and leaders in their own rights. However, women as managers face a long uphill path and with little or no support from the society, management and from within the family. For women, to be a manager and a leader they encounter some as well as deeply embedded issues in the organization themselves.

1. Women need to have the clarity of the role definition of what a manager is. They need to explore and discover their own

language as a manager rather than getting caught and tied down with male models of managerial roles.

2. Women need to encounter the given reality that they play multiple roles in multiple systems. They need to integrate these roles and arrive at clarity of choices and roles and squarely face the dilemmas of choices.

3. The third issue is adept, adopt and adjust or redefine and redesign the existing role so that they can be effective and contribute to the systems they are a part of.

For women climbing the ladder of success to the top management level is an uphill meandering tempered with a lonely struggle. Backed by knowledge competency and skills, the women feel some of their path as well as the destination; however, there are many times when they get caught with the deeply embedded role attitudes and social and organization processes, which make them, sway from determination to helplessness.

Inhibitors to Growth

Another spectrum of women not gaining the managerial position is because of three categories of behaviour habits and styles of operating

1. Women managers are not given high risk, high profile assignment necessary for promotions, because on the way up the ladder they are cautious and avoid taking risks. Women are more cautious and more likely than men to reflect rather than to act.

2. Women concern for others and sense of responsibilities for the team can make them too detail oriented 'moving them into a rescuing and mothering mode' and not leaving time for managing the broader challenges.

3. Women who had to be tough and even righteous about their agendas in mid-level positions find these characteristics are hard to shake when they reach to the top level. They become

defensive about challenges to their ideas or agendas and too insecure to think and interact with creative flexibility.

Essentially, the women get entrenched into their initial positions of anxieties and insecurities and find and difficult to relocate themselves in their achievements, accomplishments and success. Unless this takes place, women would find it difficult to grow and earn the respect of the group of the organization.

To be successful women managers, women needs to shed the deeply embedded baggage of the past as well as own up their courage convictions and work with analytical as well as rational abilities. She needs to be more responsive to the challenges and accommodative as the managerial scenario is unpredictable and tends to be in a flux and constantly reconfiguring. It is in this ambiguous pace that she will find the new road map to charter new path for herself.

However, various studies show that the impediments in the path of successful women managers are many. Male colleague believe that their female counterparts are soft in decision-making. Similarly there is a common belief that the women are far more emotional and can get swayed when there are tough decisions around tasks and/ or human consideration. However, these are the unique resources and strengths of women in a highly task and achievement and targets and result focused organization. These emotions need to be channelized in the right directions, which will enhance and strengthen women ability to be more perceptive, more friendly and aware of people around them. Organization need to ensure to translate the resources of women to transform the organization into both task and result focused as well as sensitive to the human aspects without compromising either.

A common criticism about women manager is that they are not good leadership material as they do not invest enough on enhancing their knowledge and leadership skills through training programs and interaction with peers. They are caught up in managing home and children in whatever time, which is available.

As quoted by one male manager:

"... the leader is always chosen not just for his performance but for his ability to lead a team and impart a clear vision for the organization to the team and women just do not seem to realize it because their energies are focused on just superior performance of the job at hand..."

Such perceptions and other self effacing evaluation will remain part of the organization culture as long as women, men and organization fail to accept that for women multiplicity of roles are a reality and the organization need to facilitate such role taking processes. This is possible only when men also learn and accept the social role responsibilities as legitimately part of their roles to create a home and manage family.

Such criticism disheartens or creates anxiety in women. This also does not let them own up and enjoy their achievements and success. Women managers need multi-source support from the family, neighbourhood and from the organization. Without their support women manager's struggle becomes harder. By supporting women's entry and integration in work as a part of life and not separate from it, the organization will create a diverse working environment, with gender equality, gender equity and fair and just process for everyone in the organization.

Roadblocks to Growth

Major roadblocks for women who aspire to achieve and succeed in organizations are the presence of social and role of constraints imposed upon them by society, the family and women themselves. These constraints, are referred as myths fostered and sustained with preconceived ideas and unsupported evidence, which generate guilt in women.

Myths Applied to Women in Business

1. Women switch jobs more frequently than men
2. Women would not work if economic reasons did not force them into the labor market
3. Women fall apart in a crisis
4. Women are too concerned with the social aspects of their jobs and cannot be trusted with important matters
5. Women are more concerned than men about working conditions and they are not willing to travel extensively for the organization

Many of these stated attitudes are still prevalent within the corporate structure. Women must be equipped and prepared to encounter these attitudes as they grow in the corporate level. Women managers need to go into their jobs knowing that there will be some barriers. They will not receive a welcome when they are making drastic and dramatic departures from the well-defined social roles. However, they also need to be aware of the fact that across time women have broken the chains and shackles of centuries and that they have the capabilities, abilities as well as intellectual competency to achieve success as well as retain their own identity.

Although the number of women in the work force has increased and will continue to increase in the field of governmental service and in educational area, the advancement of women into the management has not kept pace with the increase of working women. The reasons are:

1. Society has its own stereotypes and biases against women in executive positions. Women are viewed as fragile and lacking in the qualities that are considered beneficial to be effective managers. Traditional masculine traits have higher perceived value than the feminine traits in management world.
2. The position which the individual hold within the organization shapes the traits and the behavior they develop or posses. Women often secure positions that have titles with little real power or supervisory authority.

3. Mentoring plays an important role in the advancement of women into management positions. However, mentoring are often limited for women, which in turn results in a lack of access and training that aids in advancement within the organization.

4. Women managers had to face the glass ceiling. Majority of women because of glass ceiling are unable to advance in their career.

5. To complicate matter worse, women often have to deal with the complexities of the dual role as working women and mother. Women stereotypically have the roles running the household and raising the children. Such duties take away from the time, which the women can spend on the job subsequently, which slow down their careers. Women managers with children are often looked on less favorable than those without children and they are viewed as being less committed.

6. Lastly, women managers also have their own inner battles, which need to be fought and overcome. Women need to develop the confidence and appropriate skills and attitudes which are needed to succeed in business. Women manager needs to establish their career goals and acquire determination to overcome the obstacles that exist to keep women from accomplishing their goals.

However, in order to overcome such insurmountable obstacle, women need to seek support. Success today requires organizations to best utilize the talent available to them irrespective of the gender. To do these, barriers to upward mobility for women needs to be removed. Organizations need to redefine and restructure the organization systems to respond to the dilemmas faced by women managers. Organization has recognized that female executives offer a wealth of talent. Often women become 'Super Woman' to respond to being equal.

The striking part of women managers is that they are very good at juggling around the tasks. One of the strongest skills is their ability at multi-tasking. Also women managers bring with them a different style and different skills. Research also confirms that women managers see things laterally, intuitively and differently. They can handle more contradictions, can tolerate more and deliver much more than men.

The belief that women managers are uncertain of them, look for constant reassurance and tend to be aggressive are stereotyped responses which feed and multiply on themselves. The reality is that women in general and women managers in particular have a different value system, which they bring to the organization.

For women managers it is truly a case of twice the work and half the reward. It is a trying process for women to prove one again and again. However, women do feel that it is unfair to brand them as 'women manager' or to compare them with their male counterparts. Women have journeyed a long distance to enter the corporate boardrooms, take the leadership roles in organization and institutions and work as managers and employees across the levels of hierarchies in the organization. However, when we look around it is also a glaring fact that nothing has changed so far for million of women across the world where they live with the baggage of past traditions and are still shackled and chained by the traditional role definitions, which are compulsive and oppressive and which gives them no space and identity to be themselves.

In any case, emphasis must be laid on the delivery of work and shouldering of responsibility and not assess quality or results by gender differentiation. Ultimately, it lies in the hands of women and enlightened men at the helm of organization to ensure that the people are employed on the basis of their merit and competence and not because of their gender.

Exploring how the woman of today has travelled a long way and has created a niche for herself both at the home front and at the workplace, we examine the space she has created for herself. We explore how women in organisations have managed new roles, given shape to new patterns of identity and met challenges of the new millennium. Let us examine the five phases of evolution, spanning five decades, each describing the

Indian woman's role in management as well as future opportunities and challenges.

Phase I: Women in the Fifties

The women of the fifties can be categorised based on their reasons and motivation for joining the workplace. Women entered the workplace for two different reasons. Some women chose the work option primarily due to economic considerations and monetary reasons. These women were educated and the families required the resources. A different section of women belonged to families that owned businesses or were well placed in professional circles. The women were educated, were not compelled to do household chores, were intelligent and capable and wanted to utilise their education to pursue professional activities. Some women entered the world of business due to the loss of a male family member. These women took the dual responsibility of income generation and home management. A number of these women took on marginal and infra-structural service roles. In their attitudes, they brought the baggage of social structures and familial roles. The organisation and the men within the organisation also related with these women by locating them within familiar societal structures and social role expectations. These women, men and organisations focused on the job but also related with each other as per the coding of traditional social roles. As such, these women who had entered the workplace for the first time held on tenaciously to whatever organisational role that was available, and tried to contribute their best. They dutifully fulfilled social role responsibilities and sought a sense of fulfilment in their accomplishments. However, they remained caught between the pulls and pushes of the both systems.

The professional history of several of these women suggests that they did not rise in the hierarchy of the organisation and remained entrenched in a particular supporting role or function. Women found it difficult to exercise legitimate functional authority, either downwards with their male subordinates, or laterally with colleagues for effective performance. They could only plead, cajole, persuade and use social skills to get tasks done. It was difficult for women to have a similar career path as that of their male counterparts. Existing cultural and societal patterns of gender discrimination continued to make inroads into the evaluation and promotion policies of the organisation. Consequently, many women carried great responsibilities without a corresponding designation in the organisation. These women in management were considered reliable and dependable and were indispensable in the organisation. Like the social system, women were also taken for granted by the organisation. On their part the women contributed to this situation by assuming the role of a dutiful and submissive person rather than asserting themselves and demanding what was rightfully theirs. That was to come later.

Working women managed the home and stretched to fulfil all their social role obligations. For these women, it was unthinkable to state that they were often extending and stretching themselves. However, they hoped for societal understanding of their aspirations and support for their personal and professional roles. They did not ask for help either from the husband, the in-laws or the children. Children continued to be brought up in the traditional way. Children created guilt and anxiety in these women, feeling that their mothers were not like other traditional mothers. The husband and the extended family continued to expect that the woman fulfils all her traditional social roles. To them her work was a luxury and a privilege granted by the family and which could be taken away if traditional roles were not satisfactorily fulfilled.

These pioneer women were the first entrants in the Indian workplace. They discovered that work provided a meaning to their life and highlighted a new facet in their personality. This new found personal meaning created anxiety in the social system. The women themselves experienced work as a privilege and as an opportunity which many others of their ilk did not have. They had a job which gave them confidence, a steady income and the opportunity to make good use of their education. The first generation working women were forging a new role and a space for themselves and were also charting a path for women of future generations.

Phase II: Women in the Sixties and Seventies

By the mid sixties, women in significant numbers had entered the portals of formal education both at the primary level and at higher levels. In the realm of work, new frontiers had opened up for women. These women had grown up with the benefit of education and dreamt of a different role and life for themselves. Upon graduation, they entered organisations in significant numbers and aspired for career growth. This was quite unlike their mothers who were housewives or the women in organisations before them who were satisfied with whatever responsibilities that were assigned to them but did not actively seek career paths. These were the "second generation" of working women who were benefited by the trend set by the women who had entered organisations in the 50's. It should be mentioned that the reference to this "generation" of women is only symbolic. Women entering organisations in the sixties belong to the second generation in the sense that women in the fifties had already set the trend hence, the problems that these women of the 60's and 70 have encountered were considerably fewer. Women in the 60's and 70's had aspirations to perform and be rewarded, could walk alongside men and could deliver results without seeking the privileges of feminine social roles. They were willing to stay longer hours at work, perform and prove their capabilities. They also demanded that the organisation reviews policies and takes stock of women's contribution rather than merely assigning responsibilities and relegating them to marginal infra-structural roles. For example, men at the workplace as well as the husband at home were comfortable with women engaging in secretarial jobs or what they perceived as 'soft ' organisational roles such as office administration. However, more 'aggressive' roles such as a woman banker or a female marketing manager were considered suspect by the male orthodoxy.

In this phase of the country and its history, education provided an increased knowledge base for both men and women and organisations experienced unprecedented growth opportunities. This landed increased momentum to the career paths of employees. Some of the new realities of women in management in India in this phase reflect the following patterns:

- Women regarded work as an integral aspect of their life.
- Both income generation and career progression were considered significant.
- Educated and qualified women aspired for multiple roles vis-à-vis their mothers and grandmothers. These women wanted both – home, marriage and children, as well as a career.
- These women accepted the traditional social behaviour from the older generation but from their husbands, colleagues and children they expected understanding and support in their careers. They looked for re-definition of personal roles and of societal systems.
- In managerial roles women were willing to do their share of work but also wanted participation in policy formulation and decision making. They wanted their voice to be heard as stakeholders and managers of the company.

In essence, the women of this era who entered management sought jobs and careers which gave significant meaning to their lives. A career was not just a job to manage boredom or put education and investment to good use. Work was significant in itself. Moreover, working women had acquired an immense significance in the social system. A job was a life time income generator, and an insurance policy against mistreatment by the in-laws. A job had also become a means to gain societal respect and to achieve self-reliance. The extra income also added to the social status and quality of life of the extended family.

The women in this phase were beginning to forge a career for themselves, but had no female role models. They made successful men as their role models. Many women learnt to be assertive and sometimes aggressive. They became ambitious and competitive. Many women were willing to give up marriage and devote most of their time, effort and energy to professional success. Some women who were married and had children, experienced problems with their spouses as well as children who were not prepared to accept the new person that she was transforming into. The husband and children intellectually accepted and understood the change but found it difficult to realign their traditional expectations. The society at large was undergoing a period of transition. Women of this era were not only defining new roles for themselves but were also catalysing societal transformation. However, one thing was clear. Many women had to pay a huge price due to the absence of female organisational role models and the consequent emulation of successful male colleagues.

Commonly, men at the workplace were anxious and apprehensive about women's emerging ambitions and aspirations. In turn women were also unable to own up or relate to their own femininity. Women experienced their femininity as a liability and pushed it aside. Many searched for meaningful and satisfying relationships but ended up lonely and isolated. This further pushed them towards work and created a thirst for achievement and success. The social structure and processes however, did not keep pace with the emerging realities of women and their career aspirations. Familial expectations also continued to be anchored in traditional social roles and responsibilities. There were endless debates within the family about the fate of children growing up without the continuous presence of the mother at home. Any reference to the enhanced quality of life brought a retort from the family that it was not necessary for women to work.

A significant number of women of the 60's and 70's graduated from junior management levels to enter middle and senior levels of management. The female contingent at middle management organisational levels was further reinforced by highly qualified post-graduate women entering the organisation directly at responsible management positions. These women were equipped with management knowledge, skills and techniques. As stated earlier, education proved to be the major enabler for success. Women began to earn the respect of their superiors, colleagues and subordinates. Women in senior professional positions resulted in the dilution of gender stereotypes and myths about what women could achieve. There was a sea change at the organisational level from scepticism about working women to acceptance of their rightful location and space in the corporate world.

Phase III: Women in the Eighties

This was the era of emerging professionalism. Women of the fifties, sixties and seventies had accepted both their social and work roles. They played the social role in the traditional mode and to some extent carried that to the organisation. They rode two horses and juggled seemingly conflicting roles. The stereotyping of men in 'successful career paths' meant that women had to surrender their femininity and sacrifice personal lives and relationships. Some women experienced motherhood as a chore and a responsibility that was not adequately shared by the husband. This created the dilemma of choice between the traditional feminine role and the role of a working woman. It created two different siloed worlds that were difficult to bridge. The early generations of working women experienced alienation from both worlds without the fulfilment and rewards that each had to offer. This created a schizophrenic psyche which was neither feminine nor masculine. Women ended up emulating male managers. For many women, work was necessary but marriage, motherhood and social relationships were equally important. The women of the eighties attempted to bridge this dichotomy and to lead wholesome rather than fragmented lives. They attempted to broaden their personal vision to encompass both career goals and familial relationships. The women of the eighties had invested in themselves, designed multiple roles in their lives and learnt to manage their home and work interfaces to respond to available opportunities and challenges.

A major difficulty faced by women of the eighties was the dilemma of "either or" choices. When women have moved from the location of a job orientation to a career orientation they believed that their social roles and systems and existing relationships were to be sacrificed.

They postulated and often rightly so, that the social systems, roles and relationships anchored in traditional culture constrained their career growth. Confronted with this "either or" situation many women opted for limited job orientation and remained rooted in social systems, roles and relationships. Therefore, women who chose a career path believed that the choice of a career meant sacrificing a part of themselves and their identity. They either had troubled marriages or experienced upheavals in their personal lives and in their roles of wife and mother. They tried anchored themselves in their professional work and career. This often left the working women feeling denied and deprived of their multiplicity. They used the organisation for their search for personal meaning and fulfilment. Organisations by their very nature cannot be the totality of an individual's meaning and fulfilment. In our view, the concept of personal sacrifice as the only alternative for career choice has its genesis in the cultural and social milieu. There has evolved over centuries the concept that the culture and society in India have contributed to the constraints that women experience in their lives. This belief may have some truth in it but it is not the total reality. There is a need to examine the strengths and the positive attributes of Indian culture. The historical backdrop and socio-cultural framework need to be re-examined for a more realistic appraisal of support systems and positive aspects that working women can draw upon. The search of the working woman for multi-dimensional fulfilment continues in the 90's where we witness resolution of several of these dilemmas in the lives of the daughters of early generation working women.

Phase IV: Women in the Nineties

The women of the nineties emerged as a qualitatively different breed of women. The upbringing and education of women in the nineties have been different than what it was for women of the prior generation. Women in the nineties increasingly have role models anchored in their own gender – mothers, aunts and teachers who had successful careers and who inspired the young women of today to take up new challenges, explore new vistas, compete at the workplace and find personal fulfillment. Over time the education system in India has evolved in terms of fairness and support towards female students. The generation of women growing up in the nineties have also had support from the males in the family, i. e., the fathers as well as other males in the primary system. This attitude of openness has facilitated women both at the social as well as professional levels. The daughters were encouraged to be financially independent before they contemplated matrimony. Financial independence resulted in self-reliance and conferred equality of status at the social level. Gradually men began supporting the career aspirations of women and began accepting them as their equals. These men opted for educated and intelligent women as a life partners, and accepted that women require their own personal space for their growth. A transition and a transformation are occurring in Indian families, particularly in metropolitan cities.

Women of the nineties have performed exceedingly well in professional organisations through determination, assertiveness and commitment to work. They developed better relationships with their colleagues laterally as well as vertically and contributed to the overall collectively of the organisation. In addition, organisations acknowledge management qualities of women such as patience, tolerance, honesty, loyalty and communication skills. Moreover, it is also believed that women have to work twice as hard to prove their capabilities and worth. However, one must also recognise that in any organisational work setting the men also have to prove their worth to be respected for their competency and capability. As such, in the organisational context both women and men need to prove their capability and competency through performance, achievements and results. The unique dimension of women is that they struggle with the dilemma of choices between motherhood and work roles. Often her logical faculties coupled with her sense of commitment pulls her to a professional choice whereas her heart as well as her role as a mother pulls her to the child, especially an ill child. In this process, the child also does not make it easy for the mother as the socialisation of the child is coded in the social role of the mother providing the nurturing. The child also senses the guilt and dilemma of the mother and becomes anxious.

In the emerging business environment the challenges facing the Indian women of today include the need to manage multiple roles and to remain competitive at the workplace. This "survival of the fittest" syndrome in the organisational context means long working hours. Given the fact that there is increasing acceptance of women in organisations as well as greater professional opportunities it is still difficult for the women to reach the top. Working women constantly juggle roles and attempt to maintain a balance between home and a career. Their path is uphill and immensely difficult. The path is not made any easier by the many colleagues who are still caught in the traditionalism of their own roles, as well as those who are using social structures for their own convenience. The organisations which attempt to provide facilities for women raise the reverse comparisons of working women having a favoured or privileged status as compared to men who also have working wives. The organisations may not be sensitive to the issues of dual career couples, while they may be sensitive to the specific social issues of their female employees.

Today's better organisations have attempted to understand the issues faced by working women and to address these issues realistically. There are many organisations where women feel safe, secure and respected for their capabilities and the managerial roles they play. Our attempt here is not to present a bleak scenario which stereotypes the difficulties faced by women in management but rather to identify the dilemmas that these women encounter. If indeed these are the realities of the changing environment, then women in management have the possibility of transforming and redefining the organisational context as well as their roles within it. As the number of women in organisations increases, there is an emergence of a critical mass of women in management who can compel the organisations to look at different ways to facilitate female employees. For example organisations are looking at the concepts of flexi time, maternity leaves, part time work, home offices and similar mechanisms to ensure that women managers are productive while at the same time not alienated from their familial commitments. Indeed, with the increasing number of working couples there is a need for organisations to become increasingly sensitive to both male and female employees. Issues faced by working men, particularly those with professional spouses are no less stressful and need to be addressed through paternity leaves, flexible working hours and such other mechanisms. These enabling measures for employees are increasingly possible due to the IT revolution that has taken place in India.

Women in the nineties have become conscious of the voice of their own identity. With economic independence, women have acquired self-esteem and have also discovered that they are able to deal with situations single-handedly. When confronted with difficult situations such as forced marriages, domestic violence, demands for dowry, forced conformity to traditional roles and other forms of psychological harassment, women increasingly stand up to their rights and assert themselves. In general, the women of the nineties are increasingly aware of their right to choose and to shape their own destiny. Many women have learnt to live alone, travel alone, and rear children alone if marriage fails. Some women have preferred to remain single and are leading fulfilling lives. Many working couples have opted to remain childless, indicating a departure from blind adherence to traditional societal expectations. Others have chosen to limit their families to one or two children in order to better achieve professional as well as personal goals.

Although the world on one hand has reached an era which is progressive and forward looking, there still exist a number of people in the society who cannot cope with the thought of women stepping out of the portals of their home. Such people either hamper the professional growth of women or cast aspirations upon their motives. Many women have learnt to fight back, but others who are docile and timid tolerate such indignities due to financial constraints or fear of confrontation. On the one hand there is a progressive scenario for the today's women, while on the flip-side there is the traditional Indian society within which both women and men live by deeply embedded social norms. Change is evident, but the transition of women from the traditional mould to a system which allows freedom of choice needs to be expedited. Moreover, progressive attitudes need to be extended beyond the educated elite.

Phase V: Transition to the New Millennium

The decade of the nineties witnessed a major paradigm shift in the business environment in the country. The shift is away from industries based on manufacturing towards industries offering services. The service industry lends itself to a more flexible work ethos, one that allows individuals to be part of the work force regardless of their geographic location and work schedules. This trend has been reinforced by the widespread availability of enabling technologies, such as user-friendly computer hardware/software, internet facilities and virtual libraries. These industries have also been extremely profitable and have created phenomenal opportunities for the proper utilisation of the significant human resource that is available in India. These are industries that are new and vigorous and do not suffer from the baggage of the past.

Women have the opportunity to create virtual working environments at home, avail of flexible working hours and therefore better deal with social and home responsibilities. The emerging scenario in the new millennium suggests changes at the workplace which were unthinkable in the past. Some of these are found below:

- The new work environment will also enable men to enjoy various flexibility in their work schedule and they will therefore also be able to participate in activities such as bringing up children and cooking, which were previously considered to be exclusively the women's domain. Parenting would acquire significant focus.
- The Y2K women will have outgrown the rebellious phase in her quest towards equality, fulfilment and self-actualisation.

She will not only be an equal contributing partner at the workplace but will also enjoy and partake of the joys of marriage, motherhood, partnership and other activities in the social milieu.

Another possibility is that the geographic reach of women will be considerably enhanced due to improved technologies related to travel and communication. Perhaps marriages might evolve in a manner that spouses may live in different cities and still be able to be together for periods of time. We believe that the next century will witness increased experimentation, new ways of looking at things and destruction of old dogmas and myths.

- People will wish to try and create new things and define new roles for themselves and may want to experience innovations themselves rather than rely on "wisdom" passed down by prior generations.
- One can expect and be hopeful that changes in women's roles, identities and attitudes at the workplace and home-front will increasingly become balanced and aligned. This will make the pulls and pushes between the priorities of home and work redundant.
- One can also hope that women will be able to better deal with issues of leadership in the organisational context, by discovering wholesome ways of managing their personal dreams and career paths. Women can deal effectively with the processes of socialisation both within the family and at work, by crystallising their own identity and by taking charge of their own destiny. These changes will result from increased maturity and understanding rather than the reactionary outbursts which were characteristic of the earlier century. Women anchored in the earlier female liberation movements will become rebels without a cause. In the new age, there will be real change and catharsis after the rebellious stage witnessed during the latter half of the 20th century.

In this chapter, we have explored five phases of movement of the woman's role starting from the fifties, leading to the nineties and entering the new millennium (The Annexure summarises these phases). The movement from the fifties to the new millennium is not just a series of events over half a century but rather a transformation of mindsets and institutions which have a long history of over five thousand years. We have explored identity patterns for women of the new age below.

New Patterns of Identity for Women in the New Millennium

The transition to the new millennium is witnessing the woman of today creating new paradigms in terms of being fully engaged in multiple roles and deriving fulfillment from each of them. She is learning to be a daughter who takes responsibility for her parents, a wife who creates a home and a family, a mother who nurtures her children to thrive in the modern environment and a working person fulfilling her career ambitions. She aspires to find a relevance and a meaning for herself in life, accepts the uniqueness of her identity, and is willing to share her space in terms of co-holding different roles. Simultaneously, with all the dreams of togetherness, she searches for individuality, dignity and respect. She is also open to a life without marriage and parenting without a husband. In other words, she embraces marriage and parenting out of choice rather than out of social compulsion.

What should be her strategy to experience life, work, family and self to the fullest extent? How can she make more meaningful action choices in the ever changing environment? It seems that Indian men and women of the past century have failed to de-link the absolutism of role activities associated with gender. Women often get caught up in their primary biological roles of nurturing and sustaining the family. The professional career women get stuck in the dilemmas of choice described earlier. Each attempt to resolve these dilemmas sucks them deeper into the entrenchment of inter-personal relationships of their social and work roles.

Today at the dawn of the new millennium women are at a cross-road and at the threshold of a new life. They are the children of a new millennium and have the possibility to explore new frontiers within themselves and in the external environment. What choices do they make for themselves to realise their dreams and aspirations? The best alternative is for women to take an adventure and to search for their own identity. Rather than men, society or the system women need to look within, re-discover themselves and become change agents for the society. Fortunately, many women of the 20th century have taken an adventure into the unknown and have achieved landmarks in their careers and in their lives. They have had the courage of conviction to create new roles for them, to explore the meaning of their existence and to forge an integrated identity which includes the multiple facets of social and work roles. They have claimed their existential and psychological identity beyond the social roles.

The future scenario for women in India is to walk an uphill path, to transcend the monolithic social structures and to catalyse change in the culture, the organisation and the social systems. The women of the new millennium will influence the social structures and culture by presenting a new role of being a professional, a new kind of a daughter, wife and mother. The new millennium offers a space beyond the present horizon – where, instead of hope there is active engagement with the world, instead of dreams there are commitments, instead of aspirations there are choices, instead of ideals there are convictions and instead of searching for bestowal and affirmation there is the acknowledgement of one's own unique identity. The new millennium Indian women will have to take the lead from where others left off and chart a new course for themselves. They will have to discover, encounter and live life with excitement and enthusiasm. It is trust in the self, dependence on inner resources, courage to journey forth in new territories, to live through the terrain of uncharted land that the women of today will shape their new identity. They will discover the voice which has been silenced for centuries to sing the songs of life and experience the beauty around.

The women of today will discover the magic of enlivening themselves and say, " I have travelled thus far, there are further distances to travel but there are also moments in the here and now where I can be and become". In this statement the past, the present and the future will merge to create that space where movement and stability, where noise and silence, where light and darkness, where chaos and tranquillity lose their absolutism to create a new rhythm and unfolding.

Annexure: Five Phases of Movement of Women Managers in India from the Fifties to the New Millennium

Phase I (Fifties)	Phase II (Sixties and Seventies)	Phase III (Eighties)	Phase IV (Nineties)	Phase V (Transition to the new millennium)
Job/Career orientation • Educated, waiting for marriage as per family expectations	• Educated with aspirations for career and growth	• Career was an accepted dimension of life	• Career ambitions and well defined goals. Search for personal fulfilment	• Education and career as a natural process of growing up. Movement towards developing multi-dimensional personality
• Desire to use time and education productively	• Regarded work and career as an essential aspect of life	• Created the acceptance of work role and space in the larger social, cultural and external environment	• Takes up challenges, explores new vistas, competes with men on their own turf	• Enabling technologies create new opportunities and facilitate working women

Phase I (Fifties)	Phase II (Sixties and Seventies)	Phase III (Eighties)	Phase IV (Nineties)	Phase V (Transition to the new millennium)
• Grateful to in-laws for permission to work	• Career was insurance against mistreatment by in-laws	• In-laws started accepting and taking pride in daughter-in-law's new role	• In-laws appreciating the enhanced quality of life due to working women and providing support systems. Women continue to grapple with guilt in terms of parenting and family roles. Movement from nuclear families towards small joint families or other types of support systems	• Women working from home, or taking up part-time jobs or working flexi-hours, less dependent on familial support systems due to flexible organisation structures and enabling technologies. Emergence of secondary support systems
• Job oriented	• Transition towards career orientation	• Career oriented. Emergence of the female professional	• Multifaceted personality. Career development as well as ownership of personal roles and responsibilities	• Overall fulfilment in different aspects of life, increased sense of societal responsibility. Transition from "me, myself, I" towards a broader perspective

Phase I (Fifties)	Phase II (Sixties and Seventies)	Phase III (Eighties)	Phase IV (Nineties)	Phase V (Transition to the new millennium)
The Balancing act • Gave up job after children – dominance of motherhood	• Income and career both were significant – balancing act of motherhood and work roles	• Dual career couples result in role re-definitions. Enhanced quality of education for children	• Searches for job-satisfaction and fulfilment of her aspirations and dreams	• Fulfilment both in career and motherhood. Aware of choices including the right to exercise those choices, such as marriage, child-bearing, single parenting, etc.
• Discrimination at home and at the workplace	• Pressure from families continues	• Transformation of barriers into opportunities	• Support systems at home and at the workplace	• Self-contained and less dependent on support systems.
• Feelings of guilt and anxiety	• Income adds to social status – Dilemma of choices	• Traditional systems co-exist with new roles	• Balance between home and career. Enhanced self-esteem.	• Makes new choices with confidence. Anchored in self.

Phase I (Fifties)	Phase II (Sixties and Seventies)	Phase III (Eighties)	Phase IV (Nineties)	Phase V (Transition to the new millennium)
• Pushes and pulls of two systems	• Guilt, fear and anxiety about personal roles. Rebelliousness created stress	• Demanding at both the workplace and at home.	• Better understanding and accommodation between spouses . Achieves superior quality of life due to increased opportunities, enabling technologies and support systems	• Bridging the gap between home and career through information technology and virtual organisations.
• Hangover of social roles at the workplace	• Competes with men and becomes aware of rights	• Struggles to do justice to seemingly conflicting roles	• Enhanced self confidence and self esteem. Fully engaged in multiple roles	• Gains larger perspective of life. Looks inward for strength and catalyses change in the external environment

Phase I (Fifties)	Phase II (Sixties and Seventies)	Phase III (Eighties)	Phase IV (Nineties)	Phase V (Transition to the new millennium)
Organizational experiences • Did not rise high in the organisation's hierarchy	• Began to participate in management and in the decision making at the workplace	• Corporate membership was legitimately seen as their role. Demanded their rightful place in the corporate hierarchy and in policy formulation	• Due to intense competition women had to struggle to reach the top. Inspite of that very few have reached the top coveted managerial positions	• More and more women will be able to succeed and reach top positions
• Held on to whatever was available	• Did not make choices, only compromises	• Acquired a corporate perspective – paid the price for choices	• Crystallisation of leadership roles for women within the organisation	• Multiple competencies and capabilities. IT is an enabler. Changing mindsets of working men and women and of the community at large facilitate progress

Phase I (Fifties)	Phase II (Sixties and Seventies)	Phase III (Eighties)	Phase IV (Nineties)	Phase V (Transition to the new millennium)
• Difficulty in exercising authority	• Became assertive and aggressive	• Torn between social identity and professional identity	• Coming of age, lesser need to rebel, more pragmatic	• Orchestrates multiple roles in family, society and workplace.
• No female role models available	• Successful men as role models	• Precedents set by earlier generation helpful. Proof of concept	• Professionals as role models regardless of gender	• Potential to be role models for future generations. Gender a non issue at the workplace

- Data for working women in India from the fifties to the eighties is adapted from Parikh, Indira. J. "Career Paths of Women in Management in India", W.P.884 , Indian Institute of Management, Ahmedabad, August, 1990 and Parikh, Indira J. and Shah, Nayna – "Women Managers in Transition: from Home to Corporate Offices, WP.No.941, IIM, Ahmedabad, June, 1991.
- A survey on working women in India was conducted by Parikh, Indira .J. and Engineer, M. F. (Details of the survey are found in Chapter 2 of this book).The data from this survey is also used in the table above.
- Parikh, Indira, & Pahwa, Kamya, 2020, Unpublished consultancy report.

Women at the Workplace: The Journey of Three Generations of Women

Introduction

India is a country where simultaneous juxtaposition of the ancient and the new, the traditional and the modern, the agrarian and the technological, the rural and the urban and the east and the west coexist. The living reality Of these juxtaposition to two-wheelers, cars and planet, and to farming being carried out with ploughs pulled by men and animals to mechanized tractors and farm equipment and to women living in purdah covering their faces from the eyes of men to women working in corporate offices taking international business decisions. This transition both social and technological confronts women across the country to take new roles and to walk new paths. This has also led to a larger number of women entering the world of management.

This century has witnessed Indian women enter new spheres of life. From being daughters, wives and mothers they entered educational and health institutions. They became teachers and nurses. Came the freedom movement and women in large numbers joined the freedom struggle.

Came time for building the nation – women joined the educational institutions and entered the fields of medicine, law, science, industry and finally made inroads into the field of management in formal work and industrial organizations.

In the first chapter we discussed the movement of working women in India from the fifties to the new millennium. We saw distinct phases in their development and in environmental settings during each phase of such development. From the tentative beginnings made by the pioneer women in the fifties we saw the emergence of the Y2K women – ambitious, confident and more in control of their destiny. These findings were based on our experiences in teaching, research, numerous workshops and case studies.

The present chapter will explore this theme further by discussing a survey conducted by the authors specifically for the purpose of receiving firsthand the views of working women of different generations who lived through the development phases explored earlier. This will hopefully, help us to gain individual perspectives of women experiencing the world from different vantage points and to run a reality check on the conclusions drawn in the previous chapter. Experiences shared by the interviewees will better help us understand the dynamics of the movement that women have experienced during the last half century. With examples, we will explore the factors and influences that shaped different generations of women who lived through this period and who helped to shape this era. Their upbringing, their adult experiences, their experiments in managing multiple roles and their quest to find a meaning in life, will be brought forth using real world examples. Commonalties as well as differences among different generations of women during the period under review (1950's to 2001), will be analysed.

To achieve the above objectives we conducted a survey of 32 women, 29 of whom were met personally for interviews each lasting for approximately 2 hours. The objective of the survey was a qualitative assessment and therefore candidates were chosen and interviewed in considerable depth and detail. Rather than asking people to fill out a form and analysing the results thereafter, we chose a different approach.

Each participant was requested to present their thoughts and views using a common frame. The participants were sent a brief outline describing the type of information we were seeking prior to meeting with them. We asked for their personal and educational background, influences of role models and their dreams and aspirations during their formative years. We also asked them about their career, motivating factors, achievements and future plans. We asked them to introspect and attempt to answer " What is my personal mission? "How do I define success?" We queried the interviewees about potential synergies and conflicts in terms of balancing their career and personal lives. We discussed interfacial issues with colleagues at the workplace and with family members at home. We finally discussed where working women of today were going and wanted to reach. We also looked at future opportunities and challenges related to working women. We attempted to chart a road map for tomorrow based on past learning's, present experiences and future opportunities.

The sessions were meditative and emotional with minimum interference from the interviewer. Most participants went back in time, reviewed and reflected upon their priorities and in many cases found this to be an enriching and cathartic experience. Therefore the methodology largely relied on one-on-one interviews with participants who had earlier been supplied with an explanatory project brief. The personal interviews were conducted in three different cities and involved a significant investment in terms of time and emotional energy from the participants. This was a fascinating experience for most interviewees, since the personal discussions evoked early memories, revived past traumas, brought back happy memories and in some cases were quite therapeutic. The sincerity and involvement of most participants was touching. The interviewees allowed the author's access to very private spaces in their lives in the true spirit of a joint exploration. Arguably, the interviewers benefited even more, gaining new insights and a sense of deep gratitude towards these wonderful women who gave so much of themselves. In summary, this chapter will provide a qualitative view of how today's women view the world from different vantage points.

We interviewed three generations of women. Generally, each "generation" represents an age group and usually also a certain level of seniority within organisations. There is of course some overlap, as well as atypical examples in terms of senior women occupying junior posts or increasingly in the nineties, youngsters progressing to senior positions rapidly. In atypical situations, the individual is grouped in a particular generation based on age. A notable feature of all the women participants was their high level of education. Although their personal backgrounds varied from lower middle class families to the affluent and privileged classes, all these women had significantly invested in their own education. The majority of these women had post graduate qualifications and many had professional degrees in medicine, social sciences, architecture, management, etc.

The *first generation* represents women who started their careers in the fifties and sixties. They are today in their sixties and seventies, many retired, some on consulting/Board positions, some involved in philanthropic/ educational work and a few fully active and at their peak of their careers. The *second generation* started work in the seventies and eighties and largely occupy middle to senior level management positions today. There are some exceptions in terms of women of this generation who have risen to top positions due to exceptional career orientation. The second generation women are largely in the middle stages of their careers although some are at earlier stages having chosen to make a later beginning due to motherhood. Still others have chosen jobs instead of careers and have determined the suitable mix of job-related satisfaction and personal life.

The *third generation* largely consists of women who entered the workplace in the nineties. More rapid career advancement is noticed, particularly in young women who have delayed starting a family or limited the number of children for their careers. Some of these young women are at junior / trainee positions but several others have reached middle management positions sooner than their counterparts in earlier times. Increased opportunities, competition, increased acceptance of working women and a growing culture of meritocracy appear to be key drivers for these phenomena. However, compared to fast track career men who have reached CEO levels or have been successful entrepreneurs in their late twenties and thirties, women still have a long way to go. However, there were encouraging signs in terms of women displaying drive and determination, starting entrepreneurial ventures and performing well at the workplace. We believe that the time is ripe for young women to reach leadership positions. The new generation women are fortunate in having more choices. They appear to be less 'programmed', are less burdened by the baggage of the past, do not feel victimised by the system and are more inclined to analyse legacy issues dispassionately. There are more opportunities, a significant increase in educational levels, enhanced media access and availability of enabling technologies that have re-defined the workplace. This is not to say that these women will necessarily make more aggressive career choices. Rather, the choices they make are more informed, more self-chosen and more creative. One also notices a blurring of boundaries between personal and workplaces leading to a more holistic approach to life and living. From our perspective it became apparent that although modern techniques were an enabling influence, a less appreciated aspect was the pioneering role played by women of generations past. We hope that young readers gain a perspective of this important legacy and historical debt to the pioneer women and indeed become catalysts for change for their daughters and grand daughters.

The authors have attempted to examine the thoughts of women interviewees across three generations, but would like to alert readers that boundaries between generations are necessarily arbitrary. There is indeed some overlap. However we believe that on balance, a temporal view serves to provide interesting perspectives. The following are the three generations of women who participated in our explorations:

1. The First Generation
- *The first entrants at the workplace*
- *Blazing new trails*

2. Second Generation

- *Walking the path*
- *Defining a new identity*

3. The New Generation

- *Synergising multiple life roles*
- *Shaping the future / tomorrow*

Given below is a grid, where we explore the three generations of women defined earlier across three stages of life:

1. **Early Coding:** Upbringing, role models and early dreams and aspirations
2. **Adulthood:** Balancing different roles and interfaces at home and at the workplace.
3. **Exploring new meanings:** Defining success and shaping the future.

Generations of Women

S T A G E S O F L I F E	Stage I	Stage II	Stage III
	Early Coding	Adulthood	Exploring new meanings
	Upbringing, role models and early dreams and aspirations	Balancing different roles and interfaces @ home and @ workplace	Defining success and shaping the future

The above grid allows exploration across generations for a particular life stage or alternatively allows comparisons across different stages of life for a particular generation. We have chosen the former approach to allow temporal progression of perspective across generations.

Let us first take a look at working women across three generations from their childhood till date. Then let us explore in detail the similarities and the dissimilarities across three generations to find out how the pioneer women blazed new trails, how the second generation women walked the path and how the third generation will shape the future.

1. Early Codings of Different Generations of Women: Upbringing, role models, early dreams and aspirations.

Parental influences were strong across generations but the type and impact of codings derived from parenting in the formative years was different. First generation women looked upon their fathers as achievers, and looked to their mothers for softer values. The professional role model was anchored in the man since most of these women did not have working mothers. In future generations strong parental influences continued, however male gender specificity in terms of 'work role models' got diluted. New female role models – aunts, working mothers, professors, etc. emerged. It was noticed across generations that role models for women were rooted in the family, school / university and workplace. Most women did not refer to successful men or women who were out of their immediate sphere of contact as role models. The male role models were primarily father, teacher, husband and boss at the work place. Few women mentioned male colleagues as role models indicating projection of the 'all powerful father figure' into later stages of life. The fixation with the male authority figure appears more dilute in the younger interviewees. Female role models begin with the mother. The senior generation look to her for softer values. Later generations perceive her as a more complete person performing multiple roles.

Female bosses and superiors are infrequently mentioned. Perhaps this is because senior levels at the workplace are predominantly staffed by males in most industries even today. All interviewees regardless of generation had role models anchored in people they had dealt closely with– father, mother, boss, husband. Surprisingly no one mentioned people they had not known like olympic stars, political figures, etc. It is difficult to read additional meaning into this without a corresponding male survey for comparison.

Among the first generation women, parents were seen to encourage the girl child to stand on her own feet. The focus was on the girl growing up to be ' independent' presumably from societal exploitation as well as undue exploitation from the husband's family– post marriage. There were virtually no female role models that parents of these girls could have drawn upon and this was a bold and unusual stance for its age and time. This is possibly one reason why career women in high positions of the first generation are few and far between. The second generation had greater opportunities to draw upon the experiences of working women in their families. They therefore did not need to overcome the first threshold and break the entry barrier. In their world, it was acceptable for a woman to work, if not for a career, at least for a living or for mental stimulation. Therefore, the seeds of reform which the first generation had sown were beginning to bear fruit. This by no means implies that there was a level playing field for women; it only means that there was a small but significant population of working women who could be identified with. The first generation women were influenced professionally and academically by their fathers, whereas softer values were inculcated by their mothers. This reflected a typical dichotomy of the times, where the father was learned in the ways of the world, whereas the mother was a home-maker by convention and not necessarily by choice. The element of choice particularly in the case of educated women was noticed in the families of second generation women, whose mothers could choose whether to work and where to work. In young girls of this generation, grandparents were found to exert strong parental influences, since in some families both parents were working. The reactive stance of the first generation i.e "my girl shall be independent when she grows up" mellowed. The emphasis shifted to facilitate the daughter's choice, her birth right to chart her own path and to achieve her own type of happiness was acknowledged by the more enlightened sections of urban society. These were daughters of mothers who themselves had career ambitions, therefore the image of the ever sacrificing women made way for a more complex and more human image.

The urge for self-expression had first been given a voice by the pioneer women. The second generation women now had the possibility to explore what 'self expression' meant for their own existence. The objective of the pioneer women was to enter the world of freedom, choice and self-expression. In other words, the mere act of donning the man's mantle was an achievement – crossing of the first threshold. Therefore, paradigms had forever changed. The pioneers had shown that women could work if they chose to. The second generation women could now tread this new trail that had been made possible and could dwell upon which choice was best for them as individuals. This is not to imply that treading the path was easy for the second generation of women. The path was unpaved and full of pitfalls. Many of the pitfalls were created by a confused society. Sure, some women could now work but who would look after the household? Who would raise the children? Who would look after the elders? Although working women were tolerated, societal expectations on the home-front did not relent easily. The male child, perennially pampered, did not easily yield his chauvinism's. Therefore the legacy of pioneer women was not an unmixed blessing for the second generation. This generation now had to deal with the societal paradoxes that the pioneers had brought into focus. The male chauvinists, the resentful elderly women who had scoffed at the pioneers of their own age, of their own era, the jealous women of the same generation who had not the opportunity to work, all had to be dealt with by the working women of the second generation.

The paradigm had been changed forever by the pioneers, but the social infrastructure and the societal transformation necessary to support the new paradigm was not in place. In summary, the changes brought by the first generation women represented a bolt of lightning, a jolt to the existing order; whereas the second generation women lived through an age of contradictions where modernism had to necessarily coexist with conservatism.

In the case of the second generation women, a significant influence of the 'working mother' – a new phenomenon for its time, was noticed. These women were deeply influenced by their mothers or by working women in their families during their formative years. For many of these women the predominant aspirations were to become a 'successful working mother'. The fact that a woman could be a successful home maker as well as have a reasonable career was in and of itself an achievement. Many had high goals and strong ambitions and had indeed reached high positions among the very first women in India to do so. However, the working mother role models and the aspect of balancing home and work were predominant themes for the second generation of women. The first generation women offer an interesting contrast. Here the recurring theme was achievement of self dependence –' women should stand on their own fact'. This was a rebellious phase in which bold initiatives were needed to do the unprecedented. Without the benefit of role models anchored in the women, working women of this generation drew inspiration from encouraging fathers and supportive mothers. The fact that a woman could go into a man's world and be his equal was in and of itself an achievement. Some of the interviewees of this pioneer generation mentioned that they had always endeavoured to do well in a given situation rather than dreaming about special achievements in future. These women strove for excellence and made the best of opportunities as they came. Multiple roles came much more naturally to the new generation women who took this as a given, therefore the dreams and aspirations of the second generation women was seen to become the baseline expectation of the new generation. The new generation women's dreams were now more clearly projected in terms of both external achievements and personal fulfilment.

The new generation working women who are today in their twenties and early thirties represent an important stage in the evolution of womankind. They are relatively less burdened by the baggage of the past, less steeped in legacy, with less need to rebel and adopt reactionary stances. Their trail blazed by women of their grandmother's era has now been paved and the new woman is at the second cross-road. Let us explore this further. By trying to break societal barriers and in paving new paths, women of two successive generations had primarily been driven by external factors. Their careers represented a cry for self-expression. They were catalysts for social transformation and architects of the emerging gender equality in the society and workplace. The young women of the third generation now have the possibility to look within. They have tremendous inner drive and the will to achieve. There was no longer the need to work as a form of rebellion or as a means to make a point. It was now possible to examine inborn aptitudes and find conventional and unconventional methods of self-expression. These women today question, "what do I want from my life? How do I want to shape my destiny? "The importance lies not so much in the type of choice but the fact that these women have the possibility to choose. We would like to caution readers that these observations are relevant to a small section of privileged, educated, urban women in our Indian society and are not generally applicable. Nonetheless we believe that these trends are important and relevant given that rural India is urbanising. It is interesting to note that less privileged women today are at a stage, the pioneers were five decades ago. This diversity is unique to developing countries given the glaring inequities that exist. The new generation, the third generation women, have the benefit of much greater exposure. They are well travelled, have benefited from secular education and modern training. The more affluent women have been educated and trained abroad. There are also increasing examples of women from middle-class families availing of scholarships for higher education in India and abroad. Also women of this generation have significant exposure to the media and are children of the information age. Information is not the exclusive domain of the privileged male child. In the modern context information is power. The new internet age has therefore changed power equations and has broken down exclusive "clubs" that had been set up for self-serving purposes. The authors would like to observe that third generation women have a tremendous responsibility, a fact that they are not necessarily cognisant of. The pioneer women shouldered the responsibility of shattering myths and fighting the establishment and thereby became trail blazers for today's youngsters. It would behove the educated urban younger women of today to take upon themselves the responsibility of opening new avenues for their less fortunate counterparts. Sadly, the sense of social responsibility towards the oppressed section of women is found wanting in the generation of today. The sense of mission displayed by the pioneer women is now replaced by self-centred attitude to life.

When asked about their dreams and aspirations new generation women were the most explicit. Their aspirations were largely centred on the self. It was also noticed in other context described earlier. These women aspired to high professional positions, and making a mark in their careers. Many had a fascination for a foreign education or for working abroad. The new generation women also had personal dreams and aspirations which they were able to enunciate clearly unlike most women of earlier generations. It is interesting to note that these women want fulfilment in both their working lives as well as their personal lives and are clear as to what they want. A certain hesitancy noted in earlier generations – hesitancy to demand for oneself, need to be seen as sacrificing rather than demanding was nowhere in evidence in the new generation. Perhaps older generations had projected the classical image of the ever sacrificing Indian woman to their working lives as well, whereas this stance does not seem to be adopted by contemporary women who were experienced to be assertive, demanding and largely self-focused. It was noted that gender specific aspirations seemed to have made way for more universal aspirations of personal and professional fulfilment and achievement.

We noticed in the first two generations a tendency towards societal service. Several participants expressed interest in the betterment of society and had made significant contributions in the field of education, healthcare, human resource development, etc. Although personal goals were important, social responsibility also came across as a dominant theme. In the new generation women the focus was more on personal achievement and self-actualisation perhaps due to the fact that the interviewees were quite young. The authors hope that this book makes a small contribution towards informing today's women of their legacy, of the sacrifices and struggles of generations past and hopefully encourages them to have a sense of mission and responsibility of those who are less fortunate.

2. Adulthood: Balancing different roles, interfaces at home and at the workplace.

The stage of life described here is adulthood where potentially complex challenges, new interfaces and indeed new responsibilities have been introduced. Womanhood, marriage, familial ties, motherhood, job, career are juxtaposed in the life space at this age. The need to balance different priorities, the need to draw inspiration from the inner self as well as other people and a necessity of synergizing different interface had now come to the fore. The participant's rich experience spanning over five decades across three generations during this phase – of being home makers as well as career women is a fascinating story of courage, will, joy and tears. Let us compare and discuss the experiences and views articulated by participants for three different generations. The interviewees described sources of strength and inspiration that helped them face challenges and difficulties.

We begin with the first generation, the pioneers. We asked the question "how do you synergise home and work?" The majority of interviewees drew inspiration and courage from their inner self. An underlying desire for self improvement and self-actualization was evident among the participants. In many instances an external effort towards self-improvement through philosophical study and self-help workshops was evident. But more importantly there was an inner drive to 'shake off the straight jacket of the past' and experiment with different roles. What was most important during this period of life was the support and encouragement received from the family. These women had encouraging husbands and other support systems within their own and their husband's families. In later years, supportive children also helped them, children who took pride in their mother's achievement. It is pertinent to note that most interviewees chosen for this project were successful working women and these women are not necessarily representative of the generation. Rather they are representative of the torch bearers of this generation. One conclusion that we can draw is that in the case of these successful women, a positive cycle of familial reinforcement was perpetuated from one generation to the next. This is not to suggest that there were no obstacles. The pioneer women were born in a societal frame where working women were an exception rather than a norm. They had to draw upon inner inspiration and courage to fight the odds. A firm determination was a major character trait common to participants of this generation. The dilemmas and conflicts faced by these women had different origins. Some originated from their upbringing where the paradoxes inherent in Indian society gave them conflicting messages. On the one hand they were encouraged by parents to educate themselves whereas on the other hand they were overprotected and denied certain opportunities by virtue of their gender. This created confusion and a rebellious streak in these women and prevented wholesome self-development.

The traditional workplace consisted of men who were not used to interfacing with working women. The coding of men particularly those of the earlier generation were inconsistent with gender equality at the workplace. Their interface with women at the workplace passed through several stages – first of non-acceptance, then of acceptance but either as a subordinate or at most as a colleague. The idea that women could surpass men at the workplace and become supervisors of men was unacceptable. When women did well at the workplace, which was often the case, some men particularly those in parallel positions experienced insecurity. Some of the women participants of the first generation reported that a woman's success in an organisation was not always perceived as merit based. Malicious rumours were spread by male colleagues who felt insecure and jealous. Single women, particularly those staying alone, were suspiciously viewed by the society. In other words, the society had yet not come to grips with the working woman and could not fully comprehend her normal and legitimate role in a merit-based, gender-neutral professional environment.

Instances where women tolerated hurts rendered to them either by their colleagues at the workplace or the husband and in-laws at the home-front were quite common. The inner strength to fight back or raise their voice was suppressed. The lessons of life taught by their parents were based on compliance, tolerance and patience. Interestingly one of the participants mentioned that women themselves might be contributing to the self-fulfilling prophecy of gender discrimination at the workplace. She related instances of women entering organisations expecting to be discriminated against and therefore presenting an aggressive stance to their colleagues. Some later realised this and introspected to find that the problem was more within themselves. This is a good example of societal codings related to gender discrimination affecting not only the male gender but also in a subtle manner the female gender.

Examining the responses of women participants representing the second generation showed interesting similarities and contrasts. The conflicts and issues of the second generation women were centred around the social role, challenges of balancing home and work, household duties and fulfilling the expectations of motherhood. Many women of this generation pursued a career, in some cases postponed marriage and in certain instances ultimately remained single. It is not that these women necessarily opted out of matrimony but rather feared loosing their new found independence, financial and otherwise. However, after attaining a reasonable level of comfort and satisfaction from work, they were open for marriage, but felt that either time had passed by, or that a suitable match was not available. Many of these women who played the role of single working women were the products of a transition phase. In trying to reach for a new shore, some lost connectivity with their familial moorings. Sometimes the baby was thrown out with the bath water. It was difficult indeed during this transition phase to achieve the right balance and the best of both worlds. There was the realisation within women of this generation of the need to explore and fulfil different aspects of their personality. There was also a grudging acceptance of this phenomenon within the urban society. However, both the women and the society did not quite know how to make conscious choices and to build negotiability between different stakeholders. There was a tendency among many women of this era to be reactive, to perceive unreal as well as real oppression by the system, and to achieve financial independence at all cost. Clearly, independence cannot exist in a vacuum and some women isolated themselves from the system rather than becoming agents of change. Societal attitudes fluctuated between grudging acceptance of the work role for women and unreasonable reactions to the natural consequences of this new order. Neither the individuals nor the society had fully grasped the revolutionary nature of the churning that was taking place and the fundamental social transformation that was underway.

We see greater clarity in the new generation women about what they want from life both professionally and personally. Many of the new generation women did not have to rebel against the system. The women of this generation are trying to find spaces of their own. Rather than professional achievement *per se* they are focussed on self-actualisation and finding happiness in different life roles–working woman, mother, wife and member of society. The interviewees of this generation were women in their twenties and thirties typically married and mothers of one or two young children. They valued and enjoyed their role as a wife and mother and also had significant career ambitions. Most were facing significant challenges in achieving both goals primarily due to recent motherhood and inequitable sharing of domestic roles by the husbands. Most had begun careers and showed significant progress. However, the pace at which their careers are progressing is slow and does not allow them to reach their fullest professional potential at this juncture. Most hoped that once their children grew up they would be able to build their careers more easily. Most participants lacked clarity that their present circumstance was a conscious choice they had made and this lack of perspective led to frustration in many cases. A dentist said, "I have the ability and capacity to open a dental clinic, but in doing so my children would be neglected as my husband works from 9 a m to 9 p m." An architect, an interior designer, a fashion designer, a gynaecologist, a human resource professional, a placement agent, an artist—all echoed the same theme. They had slowed down temporarily and were working part-time due to demands of motherhood. All these women exhibited a deeply felt sensitivity for their children, their welfare, safety and development. They were willing to sacrifice their professional ambitions for their children but did not completely want to give up their careers and erode the value of their education. They are therefore today at a stage where they are juggling both roles facing the challenges that this multitasking creates. They are trying to find solutions for the inevitable problems that arise. Comments made by the interviewees pointed to the need for a more enabling environment at home and at the work place. Well run crèches, flexitime and infra-structural support are facilitators at the workplace. Greater familial support and encouragement, as well as participation by the husband in child-rearing are enabling factors at home which women of this generation are in need of.

Although challenges faced across generations were different, the underlying personality trait was that all these women were highly ambitious. They had the power of sustenance and a burning flame within, which kept sustaining their inner drive. With each hurdle, a lesson was learnt, resilience was built and with a 'never say die' spirit they moved forward. If the pioneer generation proved to be brave, positive and spirited, the second generation displayed an ability to manage multiple roles and subtly affect social transformation, whereas today's generation is more self-centred, focussed and willing to experiment with new ideas.

Women made different choices under different circumstances across generations. There was an underlying spirit of exploration. The ability to manage multiple roles was a common trait. Some chose to perform one role at a time, some were able to master the art of simultaneously juggling multiple roles, whereas many prioritised roles during different phases of life. It is worth noting that balancing multiple roles was not a dominant feature of the first generation women. These women were highly educated and ambitious. Working women of this generation generally started their career once their children grew old enough to manage on their own. Due to support systems at home, including the joint family structure, the upbringing of children was easier. The whole family was involved in child-rearing. The child was not alone and had siblings, cousins, uncles, aunts and grandparents if their mother was working. The women still had to struggle as the path was yet uncharted. Women of this generation were hard working, sacrificing and in their later years, philanthropic.

However, the family structure started changing towards a nuclear family structure in urban areas. Typically both husband and wife worked for a living. Hence prioritising roles became essential for the working woman. The role of a mother continued to be very prominent. Second generation women, who had a job-oriented approach, working mainly for a second income did not find balancing very stressful as they did not bring along with them the stresses experienced on the job. They were better able to separate their work space and their personal space due to clear and unambiguous separation between the two. However, career oriented women were stretched between the cognitive and emotive facets of their personality. They desired a fulfilling family life on one hand and had a vision of reaching considerable heights in their career on the other hand. In such situations it was difficult to 'switch off ' after reaching home from their office and a 'nine-to-five' routine was impossible. The new generation women or the 'jugglers' as they called themselves had a totally different perspective as far as balancing multiple roles is concerned. The quest for 'perfection' in every role and the determination to get the best out of life are dominant characteristics of the new generation. These high expectations relating to all aspects of life sometimes lead to frustration and guilt feelings. Moreover, the task of balancing Eastern culture, traditions and values with Western modernism is not without its contradictions.

Building an effective interface with professional colleagues across levels in the organisation was a different kind of a challenge faced by working women. Among the first generation women, issues related to insecurity and jealousy experienced by male colleagues were pertinent. This was because women were very few in organisational set-ups. If these women held high positions the male ego was hurt. Therefore the focus was more on preservation of the prevailing status quo rather than on capability or merit. Men in those times just could not imagine reporting to a woman. These feelings of resentment by male colleagues were also experienced by the second generation women. The emerging female workforce was often not taken seriously by men and often aspirations were cast upon women who progressed in the organisation. On the positive side senior women were well accepted by male subordinates. Here the female boss was perceived as a mentor at the workplace and was often projected as a mother figure. In general, working women of the first two generations had positive relationships with their male colleagues in situations where there was a gap of two to three levels of the hierarchy either upwards or downwards. In other words, whenever the woman could be projected as a mentor or a mentee, men were comfortable. This is not unsurprising given that this was a transition phase at the workplace and working women could only be experienced through the prism of the home setting i.e., as a mother figure or as a daughter. The second generation women also experienced interfacial challenges with female colleagues. This was hardly an issue for the previous generation since women at the workplace were few and far between. As time progressed, women at the workplace assumed significance in terms of numbers and had therefore to deal with each other in different roles. Women experienced jealousy and insecurity about others of the same gender and often withheld information at the workplace to protect their much cherished turf. These women were clinging on to professional positions which they and the generation before them had struggled hard to acquire. Therefore, paradoxically one sees few examples of women who owe their success to other women. Although women could be effective mentors of young subordinates, both male and female, they experience difficulties with lateral linkages in the organisation. It was still premature for effective formations of working women to emerge. Moreover, highly successful women in the organisation did not necessarily endeavour to transform the system for the benefit of female colleagues. In a different way one sees a continuation of this trend among the younger generation women. The authors believe that this is an opportune time for women to form self help groups, become catalysts for systemic change and form effective lobbies to fight for their rights.

3. Exploring new meanings: defining success and shaping the future

It was seen that when women defined success, they defined it as per its relevance to a particular stage of life. The first generation defined success in terms of deriving satisfaction out of contributing to the society and taking social responsibility. They also saw success in terms of learning and utilising their education and keeping abreast of fast changing times. The second generation were at a stage where the challenge was co-holding roles at home and work. Therefore, the definition of success revolved around attaining balance and gaining satisfaction from achieving multiple goals. The new generation women described success in personal terms. Achieving mental and emotional happiness, financial independence, leading a balanced life, evolving, growing and striving for self-actualisation were priorities for this generation. Thus it was seen across generations that differences in priorities were related to the stage in life the participants were. The definitions could therefore undergo a change depending on the participant's quest for achieving whatever they desired as life progressed. Overall the underlying theme portrayed a picture of achievement orientation, ambition, vision and optimism for the future.

The first generation women were asked to reflect upon 'where they had reached and where did they want to reach?' Although many had reached significant positions, they did not define success only in terms of climbing the corporate ladder. The fact that they have acquired mastery over their weaknesses or had changed their perspectives in accordance with the changing paradigms; the fact that they had contributed at national or state level and were part of social organisations was something they cherished. They did not want to reach a particular formal position in an organisation but felt that they could contribute more time to social issues. Some wished to shape policy matters at the government level. Being part of the global revolution gaining international recognition was also their aim. Some wanted to meditate and spend time with their family including grand-children. The second generation women had reached high positions in the organisational context. However, they also discovered that in addition to climbing the corporate ladder it was also important to evolve as a human being. A certain level of clarity about their goals had been attained. However, when questioned as to' where would they like to see themselves at the end of their career journey? 'Most participants emphasised the importance of overall peace and happiness in life. Reaching a high designation was important to them, but was not their ultimate aim. Being good mothers to their children and leading a happy family life were priorities.

The new generation women had a well-defined mission for the future. These women wanted to turn their dreams and aspirations into reality. They aimed at reaching the top in their chosen profession on the one hand, and also desired a happy, contented family life. Both goals were considered equally important. These women are not very satisfied with the progress of their career but have developed tremendous awareness of their future mission. The initial hurry in pursuing a career and then a 'slow down' due to family responsibilities is prevalent in women of this generation. These women are ambitious and hungry for growth, both personal and professional. Their ambition is both their strength as well as the reason for their stress and frustration. There is a craving to achieve perfection in familial roles particularly motherhood as well as the desire to excel at the workplace. The desire to achieve both objectives simultaneously in the shortest possible time frame leads to high stress and occasionally to catastrophe in one or both endeavours. Due to the impulsiveness of youth these women find it difficult to prioritise and plan their seemingly conflicting ambitions. Although women are blessed with the possibility of achieving fulfilment, both as a mother and as a career person the downside for women who start a family is that their careers come to fruition later than those of men who are otherwise no more competent. We believe that these women have unprecedented opportunities ahead of them, since they have to deal less with legacy issues of the past and traditional societal issues which shackled earlier generations of their gender. Moreover, the advent of new industry sectors such as IT as well as the possibility to grow as knowledge workers in a networked environment should serve to boost the careers of working women. Another heartening observation from our interaction with young interviewees was that these women had the ability to introspect and were interested in investing in heir family life which would allow them balanced growth and a strong platform to realise future career ambitions.

In a recent article " family before career" Singh V., 2000, talks about "the growing breed of working professionals who want to accord to their families the same degree of attention that they would to their work". The article describes instances, wherein a successful lawyer, an MBA working as an HR executive, a teacher and a private banker opted out of a career for the sake of spending time with their children. These women felt that after leaving their jobs, the overall confidence, growth and sense of emotional security in their children has increased many folds. They were of the opinion that there was no substitute for mother's love. Support systems such as crèche facilities were insufficient to inculcate the right values in a child. It was believed that a rapport developed between a mother and a child changes the child's outlook that in turn learn to be confident, motivated and feel secure. All these women do have an ambition, but they have made a choice keeping certain priorities in mind. They felt that it was utmost important to be present with their children in their growing years in order to build up a better future for them. They were clear that once their children are big they could start all over again.

Most interviewees seemed more concerned with doing justice to both their personal and professional lives, rather than achieving a coveted title within an organisation. Indeed it seems reasonable to re-evaluate the traditional concept of organisational hierarchy after the emergence of women as a significant part of the work force. A simplistic concept within the 'all male' organisation of achieving a title, reaching a good post or becoming the most aggressive hunter is not entirely relevant to a work force which has both genders. We found that many women defined their professional achievement, not in hierarchical terms but in more human terms. Many women from the first generation saw the senior organisational positions they had achieved as a means to do good within the organisation and in the societal context. Some happened to be spouses of owner managers whereas others had carved out their own career path. Interestingly, younger women defined their career more in terms of self-actualisation, self-development and learning as opposed to hierarchical ambitions. This is not to suggest that these women do have not career ambitions or they do not want their just rewards. These are highly ambitious women who take pride in their achievements. However, they define success in a broad and holistic way. The authors are unsure whether these young women will encounter significant resistance at the workplace in terms of reaching top positions. Probably, some will, some won't and for many it would not matter.

We believe that the issues of the future will focus on defining success in human terms, fulfilling and synergising different aspects of life in addition to creating value for the organisation in today's inter-connected and web-enabled world.

Seven Phases of Universal Life Space of a Woman

Across time man has searched for answers for dilemmas of existence. The dilemmas of existence are around the process of living, the various phenomenon of life and the membership in multiple systems and playing multiple roles. Different dilemmas exist at different stages and phases of life. Similarly, some individuals encounter the dilemmas early in life and encounter difficult situations and dilemmas and respond to them which make them apart from the rest of the people. Such individuals are attributed the qualities of leadership where many others see and experience them as role models for their own behavior.

This approach explores the sources and why, what's and contributions to the leadership role and then attempts to identify what are the directions for an individual if he / she so chooses to grow into leadership role, or once given the responsibilities of leadership, to inculcate those qualities of leadership which would make the individual more effective and dynamic in his / her role.

It is important for an individual to first experience and articulates the dilemmas, the choices and the responses within and then take initiatives and choose an appropriate action in his / her role for the tasks and the system. Therefore, it is important to locate oneself in the ages and phases of life and the systems in which dilemmas belong and then respond. Sometimes an individual is unsure of the location of dilemmas as, the dilemmas are often intertwined within multiple dimensions. For example, an individual has to make choices in the business and the answers are very clear that the business needs personal attention, but the individual at the same time is entrapped very deeply in the issues and problems of the social system from which it is almost impossible to give time and space to the business. This dilemma does not mean that the individual does not have the leadership qualities to take charge of the business issues, but that the social system has pulled all the energy to itself and the business issues are not addressed. If the individual was clear that the business issues and the social issues are simultaneous and need to be addresses, perhaps very differently, the choices could have been made accordingly. The reality very often is that dilemmas of life which includes both social and work issues related with the relational and emotional aspects confront the individual at the same time. No dilemmas wait for one to finish and then the second one to emerge. It is very rare that appropriate sequel for dilemmas occur. They have a predisposition and a propensity for multiple dilemmas to occur simultaneously.

It is important to understand the context in which these dilemmas occur.

1. Dilemmas are around the context of belonging
2. Dilemmas are around family membership
3. Dilemmas are around relationship
4. Dilemmas are around emotional turmoil
5. Dilemmas around self and role
6. Dilemmas are around growth and
7. Dilemmas are around taking leadership roles and shaping destiny of institutions

These dilemmas are confronted by each individual when the individual stands at the threshold of taking a major step towards growth. There are some thresholds over which man has no control. These are biological thresholds when a child is conceived; the child grows in the womb. Then the child is born, is an infant, has a childhood, grows into adolescence, a young adult, to adulthood, and to maturity of age and middle age, and the old age. All these thresholds bring their own dilemmas and dynamics of growth. These are biological thresholds which an individual keeps encountering and engaging or coping with a positive or anxious attitude. However, these biological thresholds are involuntary, in the sense over this there is no control. Biologically an individual grows in predetermined way somewhat influenced by the food the individual eats and the kind of air he / she breathes and the kind of water the individual drinks. Moreover, the biological growth itself is incomplete for the human existence and therefore there is simultaneously intertwining of familial, social, psychological anchored in the cultural and societal institutions. Further, in the industrial society of more than 200 years there is a space which has been created of formal work organizations wherein the individual experiences and stands at many other thresholds which did not exist before .

Figure

There are internal inhibitors and there are external inhibitors. There are internal facilitators and external facilitators. An individual needs to recognize that the internal facilitators are anchored in the primary identity of the being of the individual just as much the inhibitors are anchored in the primary identity of the individual' non being. It is as much true of the external inhibitors which create non responses and the external facilitators which create spaces for spontaneous responses. The support of these internal and external facilitators adds well-being to the individuals and enlarges their spaces for action initiatives. These individuals who become the external facilitators for growth of other individuals and the collectivity reflect the leadership qualities. If the individual can cross the threshold of internal and external inhibitors and hold onto the external and internal facilitators in the real sense then the growth and transformations occurs simultaneously. It is the possible to take on leadership roles with maturity and sense of well-being.

An individual may believe that he / she has crossed the threshold, but may not be real then the individual takes the threshold with him / her no matter where and which direction he / she chooses. He / She has not crossed the threshold for he / she encounters the same dilemmas and situations repeatedly and echoes and shadows of people and relationships follow him repeatedly.

The model is initiated by Prof. Indira J Parikh and is meant for femaol who want to explore and discover themselves.

1. The discovery is about how they are experiencing and living their life, how they are experiencing their inner space and outer space of living and the reflections they have about the nature, purpose and meaning of life;

2. The exploration is about how they are experiencing their social space and the dynamics of relationships in the social system, their members in the social system and their interaction with each one of the relationships individually in their relationship with them and in groups;

3. The explorations are about their work space, the nature of roles and responsibilities, the interfaces across roles and people within the organization and the dynamics of relationships within the organization.

As such, this model deals with Life Space, Social Space and Work Space. Before we look at the woman's role, and identify the needs and or give descriptions and directions it is important to explore the life space and the social space. The work space comes later. In the meantime, a woman has had some reflective processes in the life space and social space. It is only in the work solace will leadership issues are taken up.

What is a Life Space?

Life Space is that space which an identity experiences for himself / herself wherever he / she is. It is a concept which an individual experiences and which he/ she engages with the world. This concept of space gets translated into social space and work space.

Life Space is influenced by life roles. Life Roles are the repeated patterns of behavior influenced by repeated similar experiences with people in his world to which the individual starts giving same or similar meanings to those experiences.

The Social Space is the space of the primary system which is the family. This is the space of all social relationships and transactions of behavior patterns among the various members of the family. The family is parental and extended family, the family is the family acquired through marriage, and creating one's own personal family of spouse and children and eventually family connected or associated from liaisons of marriage of children.

This social space is interacted through social roles. The social roles is a network of roles defined by behavior patterns and degrees of freedom of role space. The role space is also linked with responsibilities and hierarchy influencing the dynamics of relationships.

Work Space is the secondary system which an individual enters after being prepared for it. It is after the phase of education. This space converges with the social institutions of marriage and as such social maturity and occupational maturity. This space is influenced by both the Life Space as well as Social Space held by the individual.

There are seven phases in universal life space for woman

Seven Phases of Universal Life Space Grid

Phase	Age	Aspects	Detrimental factor
I	21 – 24	Pre-entry	• This group of women in the universe of completing the high school and after graduation have both the options of studying further and go for post graduate education. The women who can be called millennial are a different breed of women they have seen their mothers working and also sometimes their grandmothers working. • These women are different in the sense they are focused and have clarity of directions for their life. They are health conscious, they dress well and in a dignified manner, they speak well and are respectful to elders • These are very few women who follow this regime. However, there are a large number of women who have decided and chosen to work and manage their own finances. • The women who go for higher education are somewhat dependent on their families for resources but are committed to return these resources and many of them do return the resources taken from the families. Some go abroad and manage their own funds to help the parents. • Then there are women who have to work because of financial situation. They have studied for a purpose of getting a job, which would reduce the load on parents and the in-laws would have a working daughter-in-law who would be bringing resources and their quality of life would improve.

Phase	Age	Aspects	Detrimental factor
II	21 – 27	Entering the World of Work	• This is the universe of beyond 28 year olds. Some of the women may just be preparing to get married or so from the pressures of the parents. Some have all ready been married and with one or two children. Some may be trying hard to have a child. This universe is around marriage and motherhood and growth in the career. Women in this one's of life in the work space are beginning to show their capabilities and competencies and are in track for promotions and seem future leaders. • In the social space women managed the social relationships of the husband's family as well as the extended family. Events like marriage, illnesses and births or deaths were managed by the women, even the women who were working. Support came rarely to share the responsibilities and husbands left the management of relationships to the women. • In her life space women brought the juxtaposition of self, role, identity and her systems of home and family and work. These often were conflicting elements of growth and opportunities available to them and the surrender of their aspirations and ambitions in the name of being a good daughter, wife, and daughter in law and a mother. Women struggled to come to terms with issues of autonomy but women and men and society were unable to internalize the new coding so of the role for women independence, competence and commitment.

Phase	Age	Aspects	Detrimental factor
			• This phase of life women grappled with children, their education and the in laws and their expectations. Very often women also did the chores of the external environment which were the domain of men like taking the car for the service, getting all the gadgets in proper use and the electricians and the garage people as well as the vegetable seller, the milkman and the Dhobi and all such similar errands. Women in their search for autonomy and career were loaded with the responsibilities of both the universes but not the privileges of any. This created immense stress. • Women in this phase of life have somewhat been the beginners of millennial crowd. At one level they carry the traces in their roles, responsibilities and emotions of the agrarian culture. At another level they are logical, rational and work oriented. They are educated in the hope of working and not working is not an option available to them. As they are aspirational of rising in the corporate ladder and are aspiring for leadership positions. They also aspire to start their own enterprises or set up enterprises in partnerships with others. They come through as confident, socially skilled and are highly interactive and participative. They take the responsibility and accountability and are often tech o savvy. They are open to travelling in unfamiliar and unknown paces and manage themselves in an unknown environment.

Phase	Age	Aspects	Detrimental factor
III	28 – 35	10 – 15 years into Work Space	• The ages of 28 to 35 years you are fully steeped into work. • You have been working for a number of years and already have a history of working. You have evolved patterns of behavior of relating to people. • You also would have had several promotions. You may be preoccupied with the organization as well as your job. This is the time of new learning, developing new skills, meeting new people and most important working with a senior within organization structures of task, performance and delivery. This is a formal work organization with formal work roles operative in a hierarchical structure. By this time you would be playing out your pre-set role definitions and role maps of relating to people and situations. • Entry and settling down is the time for designing new role maps and definitions of people and situations so that you can respond with efficiency in the task, and performance and effectiveness of the role. • It is important to understand that organizations are formal systems.
IV	36 – 43	15 – 20 years into Work Space	• You are into your thirties and some of you would have entered your forties. • You would be married and many of you would have a child or two children. A decade and more has gone by. The life of carefree college and university life seem like a dream gone by.

Phase	Age	Aspects	Detrimental factor
			• Entry into the world of work is history. You are immersed in the world of work and the institution of home and family. In both the places role and responsibilities have increased.
			• By this time the children are in school, and for men the wife may or may not be working. If the wife was working and because of children she may have taken a pause from work.
			• This may create a dynamic at home. The issues of relationship between mother and daughter in law might have been somewhat at ease.
V	44 – 51	20 – 25 years into Work Space	• In this phase you are entering the age group of forties and just nearing fifties. The life space has created many diverse experiences of life for you. Some might have experienced a loss of a parent, and increased responsibilities and expectations from the remaining parent.
			• Children are into their teens and your role as parenting has decreased for them. It has also become more demanding as the pressures from the children's friends confront them with issues of right and wrong.
			• Values of the family upbringing and the culture of freedom and rebellion is confronted by you. The social dilemmas of teenagers, the technology impinging on day to day life and the generation caught up with issues in the name of freedom, all these and more are the dilemmas of this age and phase of your life.

Phase	Age	Aspects	Detrimental factor
			• Often this is the age of plateauing of relationship in marriage as the two decades milepost fly past, there might be some pause in carrier growth as well as some plateauing as well. • At this phase of your life time and again the inner need to ask oneself the basic questions of human existence. For the first time you may confront the reality decreasing years at work life rather than so many years yet to go.
VI	52 – 59	25 – 30 years into Work Space	• The countdown of how many years left to work has begun. Concerns about health and physical well-being surface very often. • The stressful life, the long hours of travel, long hours of working, the sleep deprived executive syndrome begins to appear on your face and in life. The financial concerns of planning for retirement and what will happen begin to create sleepless nights. • This is the age when ageing parents draw your attention. You are in the age group in the society where you are yet to be fully free of the responsibilities of the children. You yourself are not very old and you have ageing parents. Put all these dilemmas together you are grappling with multiple life space and relationship concerns. • At work you have reached the level of general management and or CEO. Very often you have learnt through experience from one promotion to another, but you may not have had formal management inputs. • You, who have not reached the pinnacle of success experience, a sense of futility and wonder why the destiny has been so unkind to you. You have worked hard, given your best and yet something just has not fallen into place the way it should have been.

Phase	Age	Aspects	Detrimental factor
VII	60 – 65	Life after work/Exiting from work/ Entry into new space	• This phase of life confronts you with dilemmas of disengagement from one of the most time consuming, meaning giving and integral part of your life. Your meaning has come from work. • The meaning and significance of the social status has come from work. The belonging and importance has come from the status and the significance of the organization, be it public sector, private sector, multinational and or global. • Health and the concern for health of your elders and yourself begins to creep on the surface, financial planning becomes a significant factor and the social and larger issues of family and society occupy much of the time. Children are not with you and you are responsible for two generations before. • Many of you engage and create a path of being affiliated with academic institutions where they can share the experiences, knowledge and wisdom of your lives and knowledge. While some of you may choose faith and spirituality to immerse them in contributing time, while some others plan to do Yatra and or read spiritual books. • From disengagement with work space to experience a life of freedom from work role and responsibilities, and the time and space to be with oneself and others in the management of the aging process. Departure from the work space is most of the time experienced as painful and some position of significant aspect being taken away or having to reluctantly give up.

These seven phases of life from entry into work to retirement reflects innumerable events, encounters, new spaces and new people as this is the inevitable nature of life. Each of these phases will come and go and bring you to a threshold. This threshold can remain entrenched in any time and space and that is where growth stops. Phases and stages of life will come and go, but the dilemmas will remain the same in each and every phase of life. Until a threshold is really and realistically crossed where you have to let go something, and discover something new. You have to add something from the self. It is then you truly cross the threshold and enters the next space of your life. Otherwise the threshold never leaves you. You remain in the animated suspension being pulled and pushed by the known and the familiar, and the pull of the growth into the unknown and the unfamiliar. There is also the self that has something to offer which is relevant and meaningful but, unless the pull and the push are resolved no new beginnings can be made. And once the new step is taken there is no way an individual can reopen the window or the door to old and the previous space. Once the space becomes yesterday it is but a memory and to hold onto is like a millstone around the neck. Memories are to be cherished and held in fondness and that is what gives the energy to move forward. From disengagement with work to a life of freedom from organization responsibilities to being with oneself and others in the management of the aging process needs to be attempted with dignity and grace. Looking after one's physical fitness and keeping healthy is an art and an anti-aging attitude and process.

Annexure

Unique Configuration of Women Across Three Generations

First Generation Women	Second Generation Women	Third Generation Women
Awareness among parents of the need to bring up their daughters in a manner that they can stand on their own feet.	Many women had working parents. Grandparents assumed importance in child rearing. Some women had working mothers and the first female role models emerged.	These women had unprecedented opportunity to learn and grow. They had significant exposure to the world due to media, travel and IT.
Women had educational opportunities although there was some discrimination compared to male siblings	Mothers increasingly encouraged their daughters in terms of education and in terms of pursuing a career.	Expectations of parents and society from female and male children were not as different as in the past.
Parents over protected and sheltered the female child. The child struggled for freedom.	These women had open minded parents and gradually gained opportunities for overall development. They often asserted their right to choice.	Parental influences continued to be important. However, these women had early exposure to other sources of inspiration and ideas. They are children of the information age.

First Generation Women	Second Generation Women	Third Generation Women
Female children looked to their fathers for professional guidance and to their mothers for softer values.	In their fathers they admired ambitiousness and qualities of the support and encouragement given to them from early age. In mothers, the art of balancing two roles –house and work, the power of acceptance and adjustment were some of the qualities they looked for.	Admiration for qualities in people of being self-made, independent, ethical and fair was prominent in these women. Parents of these women were open-minded and sensitive to the needs of their children.
At the workplace the first generation women had only male role models – Boss, Professors, etc.	Both male and female role models were now possible at home and at workplace. However the mentors were primarily men and were usually projected as the father figure. Encouraging husbands started becoming the norm rather than exception. However the hangover of a male dominated system persisted in extended families as well as at the workplace. Male colleagues at the workplace had yet to come to grips in relating with working women and usually tried to relate to them using social frames i.e., as father figures, brothers, etc.	At the workplace enabling technologies and more flexible attitudes within the organisation facilitated the professional progress of these women. The shift in business towards services and the growing importance of knowledge workers created new opportunities for working women.

First Generation Women	Second Generation Women	Third Generation Women
These women sought higher education but the fullest opportunity to all round personality development was unavailable. These women were strong, ambitious, patient and resilient, but lacked assertiveness.	Aggressive women were often resented and denied merit based promotions. Women started assuming male stances in order to survive in a man's world.	These women knew their mind from an early age. Globally they had travelled and experienced multi-cultural diversity. There was no need to rebel against people either at home or at workplace but they perhaps felt the need to rebel against the inefficiencies in systems as they had a comparative reference from the West.
The aspirations of these women were not properly understood by their own families as well as by in-laws. Even when families were supportive of the women's career they refused to compromise on what they perceived as the woman's familial duties.	Working women gained respect due to their professional excellence as well as the ability to contribute a second income to the family. However, societal pressures to conform persisted.	A lot of awareness was there from experiences of the former generations. Therefore synergising was much easy. Mostly the families were neutral and if joint set-ups were there , socialisation skills, tact, supportive husbands, and in-laws have eased their life roles, letting them enjoy career and motherhood both.

First Generation Women	Second Generation Women	Third Generation Women
There were conflicts at the identity level, interfacial issues with other people and the desire to rebel.	These women experienced complex interfacial issues with other women including female colleagues. Empathy for others of their own gender was often polluted by jealousy and insecurity.	These women were confident and assertive and had less need to assume a reactive or rebellious stance. However, these women also experienced instances of rivalry, jealousy, back-biting from female colleagues.
Most of these women settled for late careers after their children grew up.	Stress levels increased due to inadequate support systems for working women within organisations and at home. Multiple balances, seemingly conflicting roles continued.	Many women started their career early and deferred marriage and/or postponed motherhood. These women are highly career oriented rather than job oriented. They have a desire to fulfil both their personal as well as professional dreams. They have a zest for life.

First Generation Women	Second Generation Women	Third Generation Women
The experience of brazing a new trail at the workplace and overcoming significant obstacles was a cathartic experience for these women. They grew mentally and emotionally.	These women learnt to rebel and assert themselves. They increasingly assumed male stances at the workplace and a rebellious stance at the social level. These women represented a transition phase.	Their issues revolve more around juggling roles and in a quest of being a perfect mother, wife and a professional; they experience guilt if either of their roles is neglected due to time constraints. Also some kind of hurry is experienced in achieving everything too fast.
In later years they were imbued with a sense of mission and a desire to contribute to society. Although they achieved a sense of satisfaction from professional success their goals were not only hierarchical unlike their male counterparts. They strived for inner growth, social responsibilities and had a strong desire to contribute to social welfare.	Reaching top positions with respect to designation was not important for these women. They wanted to achieve peace, happiness and satisfaction from being good mothers, providing support to their families and also continue on the path of learning, growing and evolving themselves to a stage of perfection in whatever they undertook	Goal clarity, both personal and professional is apparent. They are also learning to manage anxieties through yoga, meditation, etc from an early age. They are inclined towards self-realisation, self-introspection and are also in turn achieving patience, resilience, empathy and maturity quite fast.

Women and the Indian Corporate World... Two Case Studies

Introduction

Women have now worked in organizations for over five decades. They have contributed to the growth, culture and performance of organizations. This reality suggests that organizations need to evaluate specific issues that confront women, men, and organizations due to women's sustained presence and increasingly higher responsibilities, decision-making roles and rise in the corporate hierarchy.

As women have risen up the corporate ladder they have acquired leadership roles and have been assigned higher organizational responsibilities. Women in leadership positions encounter issues pertaining to handling power, exercising authority, providing direction and strategic initiatives, participating in policy formulation and interfacing with the external environment. Simultaneously, women encounter interfacial issues with superiors, colleagues and subordinates of both genders. Women in leadership roles are key role-holders and encounter unique dilemmas. These dilemmas faced by women are anchored in the socio-cultural context, the organizational culture, the external business environment, as well as in their own maps and definitions of role taking. Often the issues revolve around maintaining boundaries between personal and professional roles and relationships, being efficient at the workplace and managing familial roles effectively.

We present in this paper two IIM-A Case studies.

1. Integration of women in a large fast moving consumer goods company (FMCG), Mumbai
2. Status of women in a public sector company, Mumbai.

Both studies deal with the complex subject of "women" in an organization. Issues related to employer mindsets, roles that women need to balance, integration in the organization, growth and the "glass-ceiling " effect (real or perceived) are discussed in the context of the two organisations around which the cases revolve.

Both represent two giant private and public sector undertakings respectively. Both have a long history allowing the subject of women in organisations to be explored over long span of time. Both organisations have consciously adopted policies and commissioned studies to understand the subject. The first step, i.e, the recognition of this important issue and the need to introspect , has already been taken.

As the cases unfold, readers will be taken through the issues faced by the organisation, attitudes and stances adopted by different groups and sub-groups, senior level policy decisions and the impact of policy as well as attitudinal shifts of colleagues (men and women), on women in a shared work place. The case studies identify areas where significant progress has been made, challenges for the future and the need to re-define roles.

I. The Case study of a fast moving consumer goods company,Mumbai

A) Integration of women in the company:

Women's recruitment and integration in the company during the last few years had been in small numbers. Therefore a need was felt to review the issue of women's induction, their adjustment and integration in the organisation and also their performance. Very few women were in senior positions. The company was grappling with some of the specific issues which women encountered as employees as well as in their social systems.

B) Objectives of the study:

1. To assess how women experience their entry in the company.
2. How women visualise their career path, their expectations, ambitions and aspiration.
3. Women's interface with superiors, colleagues and subordinates.
4. Appraisal of women's managerial roles, tasks, and performance.
5. Company's policies and facilities to address specific issues of women such as motherhood and subsequent break in career.
6. Women's management of work and home space.
7. Women's long term role and career path in the company.

C) Organisational Issues:

Let us examine the different issues which were a reality of this company.

1. Entry of women:

Very few women were recruited in managerial positions. At some level the company wanted to recruit women but at another level the organization's ambivalence came through. Could women cope up with the demands, challenges and pressures and would they be able to sustain their performance? This was ambivalence was reinforced by the choices made by women during the early years of their career path. Women experienced a dilemma in terms of choices around whether they should continue with their career or respond to the social roles and social systems. In terms of knowledge, capabilities and skills the women who were recruited were of the same calibre as the men. Their performance also conveyed their commitment and involvement. However, they also had to make certain choices, vis-a-vis, marriage and their social roles in homes and families.

Entry into the company was a culmination of academic performance, achievement and hard work. Women had entered with ambitions and aspirations of a career for themselves and for a career path. The recruitment was at the entry level i.e. management trainee level. The women were young, mostly unmarried and at a threshold to enter work as well as marriage. This implied that the social sectors of life for these women were going to be round the corner. Marriage and motherhood were bio-social phases of life which these women would encounter. This also meant that they would have to manage and make choices with the ambitions and aspirations of a career as well as marriage, motherhood and social roles. The company had initiated and designed some organizational policies to facilitate management of these multiple roles. But the dilemma continued to be encountered by women, men, organization and family.

Organizations that employ women have to deal with issues of task allocation, performance evaluation, education, competition, mobility, promotions and social stereotypes about women. Most women felt that expectations of the company on the job from both men and women were similar. It did not differentiate or discriminate in terms of job allocation, evaluation of performance, mobility and tasks between men and women. However, the perception of superiors, colleagues, and subordinates, about the company's policies on women was experienced differently. Most believed that there was a difference in how they treated women. The senior managers accepted that women had their own issues around work and home especially when they were on tour. As such some sensitivity needed to be extended to them and these issues needed to be addressed by the company. Colleagues resented some of these considerations extended to women. The subordinate men perceived these considerations as a privilege to seniors and specially to women.

2. Task allocation:

Women believed that the company was really not prepared for women's entry in the organization. In the factory women were treated in a somewhat protected manner. Seniors did not know how to relate to them in a formal functional relationship. However, there was lot more acceptance of women in their roles in the corporate offices. The professionally trained and educated women were ready to go in the interiors and were willing to rough it out. There was a distinct shift in women's own attitudes. They wanted to be treated at par with their male colleagues and be evaluated on their performance and merit. It was only in some of the facilities like accommodation and toilets that they were willing to accept privileges.

Women's capabilities were under-utilised. They were placed in metro cities and in large factories. Some women had a liking for a smaller factory, or a greenfield location. This was more so when they were unmarried and were not tied up with social roles and responsibilities. Similarly, the company did not allocate the sales function to women. All these underlying beliefs and assumptions about women created a context the work place where women experienced alienation from the mainstream. There was distinctly a glass ceiling which women believed they could not cross and which the organization found it difficult to remove.

Essentially, the issue revolved around the legitimacy of women's entry into formal organizations, their space and location in the organization, their job and task allocation and finally their performance evaluation. Women's social space and social role were defined by social structures and systems and they were involuntary whereas their entry into organization space and role was voluntary. Women accepted their legitimacy in the organization and were determined to be professionally oriented managers.

Figure 1

Women's Choices Between Social and Organizational Space

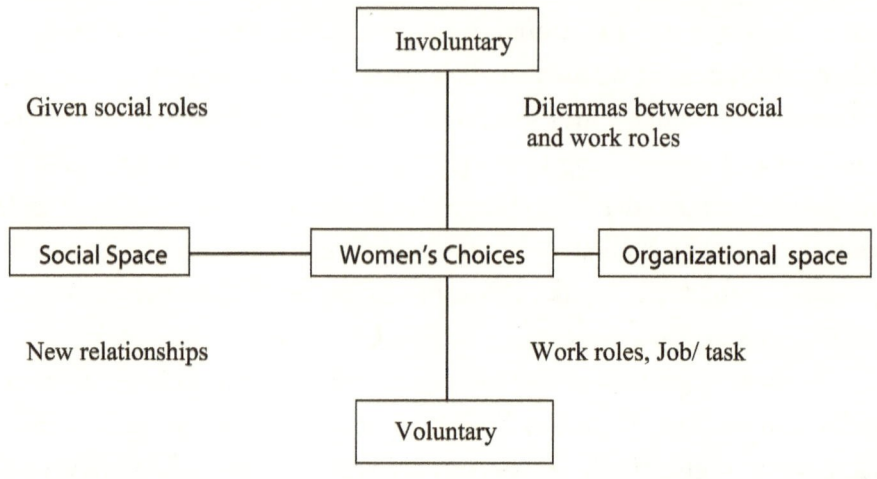

- ■ Women aspired for new relationships and work roles, with task responsibilities, career paths and corporate roles.
- ■ Yet they experienced traditional social systems and roles inhibiting their growth.
- ■ Organizations equally got caught up with social meanings of women's role and new emerging occupational meanings of women's roles.

3. Task relationship:

One of the most significant issues confronting women in management generally and specifically in the company was their relationships in the organization. It revolved around relating with superiors, colleagues and subordinates at task levels. Women found it difficult to make task demands or exercise task authority upwards with male superiors. Women found it difficult to make demands on colleagues. If they did, they were perceived as being aggressive. The social processes made it very difficult for men to accept the authority of women even in functional or task situations. Most women felt that relating with superiors was easier. The superiors treated the women with concern, stated the job expectations clearly, and were supportive. Most women believed that the seniors also wanted the women to succeed and as such encouraged them so that women and the organization both experience a sense of achievement. As far as relations with colleagues was concerned there was a lot more competitiveness. Male colleagues felt that women were provided more consideration and privileges and often felt resentful and hostile towards their female colleagues. The subordinates accepted and respected the management trainees. However, those who had risen from the secretarial ranks continued to be perceived in the earlier mode and the acceptance of role change and status of these women took a long time to manifest. The superiors, on the other hand, found women sincere, committed and hardworking. In a crisis situation , when women were confronted with performance appraisal and task demands were made, some women had a tendency to be emotional. These emotional responses of women were difficult to handle by men superiors.

The men found it difficult to handle the "aggressiveness" of women colleagues. The subordinates both men and women respected the women especially in the managerial cadre where women were professionally educated and qualified. If they performed and came through as capable and competent, the women were respected and accepted quite well.

4. Organization culture:

The most dominant characteristic of the company's working culture as perceived by women was aggressive. If the women were not aggressive they were perceived as non-effective. Therefore, most women felt that over a period of time they had become more aggressive and had lost some feminine and softer aspect of themselves. According to many women, the observation from family and friends was that they had changed within six months of being in the company. The aggressiveness was reflected in having strong opinions, getting entrenched in arguments, loosing flexibility and negotiability, showing insensitivity to others opinions and feelings, becoming closed and as such loosing openness and empathy and overall acquiring an attitude of "I know better". Women had also become more competitive, more so with colleagues. The overall company culture provided acceptance of women at a certain level of management. However, crossing the invisible threshold to senior managerial levels was difficult. Whether it was the women's membership in dual systems of family and work, and as such a break in career, or the fewer number of women at entry level, or an unconscious ambivalence from both women and the company, the fact remained that women were not in senior positions.

Another distinctive feature and perhaps found in most organizations was that there were clear boundaries between the women in management cadre and women providing infrastructural services. There was a visible difference in terms of confidence, capabilities, attire, presence and behaviour. There was a code of conduct, and an unarticulated code of behaviour which women in the management cadre followed. On the positive side the culture maintained the dignity and personal boundaries of women. Women felt safe working and had not experienced any sexual harassment of any kind. This also made them appreciative of the work and professional culture.

There was differentiation between technical, personnel and managerial positions. Though the technical people were essential, the status and significance was given to managers. This created a fragmentation in the organization between technical and managerial staff. This was further enhanced with women as part of the technical staff. The perceptions were that at some level, the career paths, opportunities and growth acquired a differential pace and the managers were at an advantage over the technical staff.

5. Women managers and men with working wives:

It was felt that the company was more responsive and perhaps more sensitive to women managers than the men with working wives. It was becoming apparent that the younger men managers had working wives, while a majority of senior managers had non-working wives. As such the senior managers were not sensitive to the issues of dual career couples while they were somewhat sensitive to the specific issues about women managers' role in the family setting.

6. Organization policies regarding women:

There were definitely some specific policies designed keeping in mind women's entry and needs which the company extended to women. These were accepted by seniors but male colleagues found it difficult to accept. For example,

1. Accommodation and living facilities were given to women earlier and nearer the office. Perhaps better facilities were also provided.
2. There were certain locations where women were not posted. This policy followed even though women posted in rural and backward areas, had performed well.
3. Flexible policies for women after child birth.
4. Contact and negotiable working hours while on career break.
5. Reemployment after career break.
6. Assisting in transfers after marriage when husband was transferred.

7. Dilemmas confronted by women:

1. At the entry level women felt that they needed to work harder to prove their competence, capabilities and be regarded as good as their male colleagues. The dilemma confronted by women was between earning respect or acceptability.
2. Time spent at work – The culture was to work late hours and on weekends and holidays. No one stated that they were required to stay late but the work culture was such. As such women felt

compelled to stay late hours. This added to their stress levels in management of multiple roles and multiple systems.

3. After marriage, management of dual systems, and multiple roles and membership requirements became the issue.

4. Pregnancy, child birth and re-entry into the work-place , had to be managed.

5. Managing the external interface of work and career, management of home, children and social roles – all became stressful.

6. Career break and the issue of seniority had to be tackled.

7. Climbing the corporate ladder and entry into senior management, was difficult.

8. Lack of formal social get togethers made it a lonely place for women.

9. As there were very few women , friendships were not easy.

10. For single women, lack of get-to-gethers and stereotyped images about single women made it difficult to build relationships with male colleagues.

11. It was a good place to work but a difficult place to have friends.

12. Mumbai as a city added to the isolation, with lack of time due to the preoccupation in managing the environment.

8. Specific issues faced by women:

1. Women management trainees had been brought up in a social milieu where it was not unusual for a women to be in formal organisations and managerial roles.

2. The women who had entered were quite career oriented women. However, one set of women felt that the priority was career, while others felt that home, family and motherhood were significant enough to give up work for sometime.

3. Success and achievement in the organization got carried over to social settings.

4. Organization structures and roles were influenced by social structures and could be constraint in work relationships and task allocation. If attitudes within the organisation were transformed, then their fullest human potential could be actualised.

5. Femininity was both a strength and a constraint for women in the organization.

D) Analysis and findings about the dilemmas faced by women with membership in multiple systems:

- Women experienced constraints and challenges upon entering the organizations. These were related to maternity leave, motherhood, demands from social relationships / systems and competition from male and female colleagues.

- Social demands such as births, deaths, marriages, illness and sickness of children and family members were the responsibilities of women. Major constraints with regard to punctuality and effectiveness were experienced and therefore this lead to stress.

- Most women felt that they could handle more responsibility and were capable of rising to senior management positions.

- Women believed they could relate more effectively with superiors, colleagues and subordinates if the organisation and the social environment were more supportive.

- Women were owners of multiple roles. The women got pulled and pushed between these conflicting roles. They were expected to be emotional in one system and logical and rational in the other.

Figure 2

Emotive – Cognitive Interface with Social and Work Context

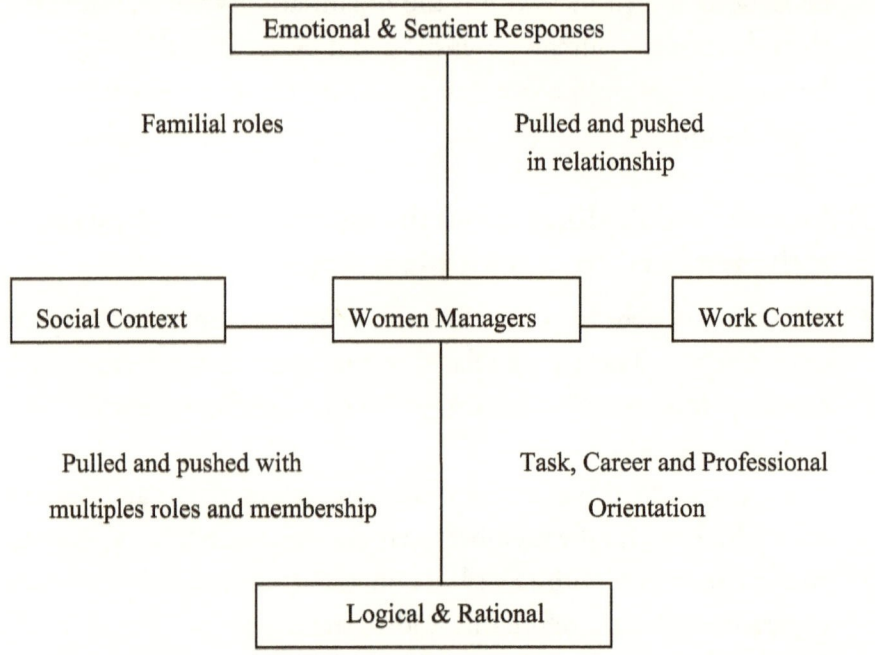

- Membership in the organization provided women with personal meaning, economic autonomy as well as self-reliance.
- However, women missed out in the security provided by traditional structures and social roles.

Often the two worlds competed with each other.

Figure 3

Women's Dilemmas in the two worlds

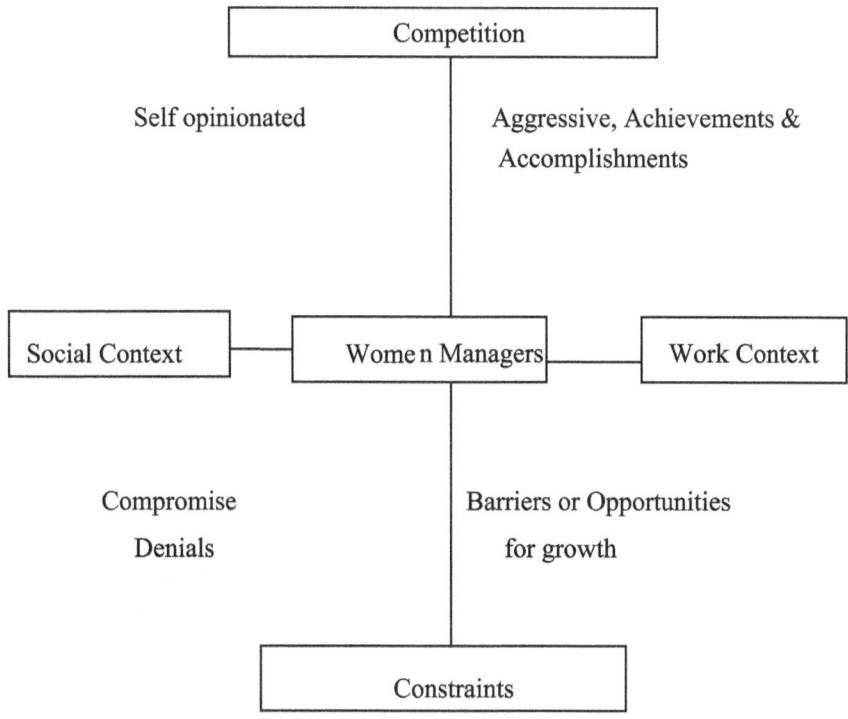

- Women had accepted the work context and the multiplicity of roles as an integral part of their life space.
- They had to deal with both constraints and opportunities and keep giving shape to their roles.

E) Future Directions:

The faculty from IIM-A after understanding the organization and its needs suggested the following directions and choices for women:

- Women carry maps and definitions of organizations. These maps and definitions of organizations would determine their roles in the organization and as such contribute to the emerging structures, systems and relationships. Understanding of the structure of the organization and its functioning could give an organizational perspective.

- The company could facilitate women to explore their roles and identity so as to locate themselves in a professional identity which is not exclusive of social identity. This clarity of location of one's identity would facilitate women and the organization to make new and meaningful responses in relationships (superiors, colleagues and subordinates) and make relevant action choices.

- Both women, men and the organisation could identify relevant characteristics of professionalism and accept the multiplicity of roles and membership in multiple systems simultaneously.

- The organisation could enunciate clear policies [and communicate it to all employees] about recruitment, induction, infrastructural facilities and support systems available to women.

- Working women and men with working wives could be provided with a basket of choices to facilitate family priorities within the framework of the company's cost structure.

- Essentially, women felt that it was a good place to work in and had a good set of people to work with . However, formulation of coherent policies by the company could create a healthy work culture and context for its women managers. New organizational models, systems and processes needed to be evolved keeping in tune with the transformations occurring in the roles of women and men and the business environment.

- Lastly, the organisation could build upon its strong work ethos by exploring transactions involving men and women and by formulating a policy framework to better integrate both genders at the workplace.

II. The Case Study of a Public Sector Undertaking, Mumbai:

A) Status of women in a pubic sector undertaking, Mumbai:

In keeping with the philosophy of Human resource development, the company had given equal status and opportunities for growth to its women employees. There had been no discrimination in terms of procedures, policies and systems with regard to recruitment, salaries, perks or working conditions. The entry of women in at the staff level began with the inception of the company, when many had retired or having become officers, were placed across the organisation.

Slowly and steadily the number of women both at the staff and the officer levels began to rise and over the years, the number stood at 2243. Women along with men employees had been utilizing all the opportunities for growth as provided by the organisation and many of the women employees, like men had also acquired an additional qualification in order to enhance their career. However no specific initiatives had been planned or identified by the organisation in the area of women's development. Neither was there any expectation by women. Women continued to experience psychological deprivation in terms of career advancement, because of their socio cultural context and history of role taking in the society.

B) Initiatives taken:

Couple of environmental factors led to the realization on the part of the women themselves as well as the organisation that the potential of women employees could be harnessed and optimized by undertaking focussed initiatives:

1. Environmental factors were:

- Opening of competition and liberalization in India brought out the fact that each and every employee of the organisation was an indispensable resource.

- Variety of strategies needed to be identified for the IOC's human resources, to enable them to meet the business challenges in the organization.
- Down sizing and curtailing of the increasing man power base was essential and measures like VRS, stricter rewards, less concessions on transfer/rotation, had to be necessarily adopted.
- Increasing number of women joining the organisation was a reality.
- Realization all over the world that women had unique strengths and certain interventions in the area of handling their multiple roles would unleash the women's potential, and, make, a tremendous difference to their contribution and output.
- Setting up of the Women in Public Sector (WIPS) forum, compelling PSU's to take membership of the forum and implement their action plan conceived for promoting the development and the growth of women employees and awards for best performing enterprise in the area of women's development was introduced.

2. Factors for Women were:

- Woman's concern, about their role in their professional job with their multiple roles.
- Personal aspirations to move up in the hierarchy and the fear about the adequacy in terms of time management and required skills.
- Women who worked with focus on economic need and no commitment to work realized that unless they took their work seriously they may become victims of voluntary retirement scheme as well as other downsizing mechanisms.
- Dilemmas of the dual working couples.
- WIPS forum encouraging women towards self development for better performance.
- Stereo-typed perceptions of men about the image of a working women.

3. Perceptions and Myths held by women, men and organizations:

- Women lacked professional orientation at work place.
- Formal work was of secondary importance to women, the primary being social and family tasks.
- Women joined work only to earn money.
- Women lacked confidence and were not assertive enough, therefore, responsible jobs could not be assigned to them.
- Women did not stay back after the formal working hours. They also refused to work on holidays.
- They came late and went home early. They wasted time in gossiping and were not available in their seats.
- Women preferred stereotyped jobs and did not come forward for challenging assignments.
- Women lacked leadership and decision making capabilities.

The company demonstrated great receptivity to the objectives of WIPS forum and displayed great sensitivity to the women's concerns and issues. Corporate HRD studied the need for designing certain interventions focussed on women specific issues embedded in the socio-cultural and occupational context, which in fact, dictated her to decide her priorities in life.

A study done on "Women's Profile" in an international workshop on "Women in Public Sector Enterprises – Current Facts and Perspectives" took into account women's concerns, experience sharing amongst colleagues and participation in exclusive programmes for women. The corporate team arrived at the conclusion that while designing interventions for women it was essential to take stock of the possible issues confronting this group. Identification of the following concerns of women which needed to be focussed are given below:

- Multiple role dimensions and expectations of women from both the system of belonging viz. home and work.
- Growing entry of educated women into formal organisations with ambition and aspirations for career advancement.

- Concentration of women employees in staff roles such as HR, PR, Finance, as well as Head offices and metropolitan cities.
- Resistance to transfers/tours and postings at field locations.
- Liberalization and competitive environment compelling the organizations to improve the quality of human resources in order to meet the challenges facing the industry.
- Resistance to attend residential training programmes or attend office get togethers etc.
- Men's perceptions anchored in the socio-cultural context.

Based on the above findings identification of *training* as one of the significant tool for dealing with above issues was undertaken. Training programmes exclusively designed for women cater to free and uninhibited sharing, interaction, and also cater to professional inputs for further enrichment.

a) The objectives while developing strategies for development and growth of women employees were:
- Facilitating integration of women employees with the company's HRD systems and policies.
- Exploring the organizational perspective and the psychological dimensions of women's role and enabling the women to deal with the demands of their multiple roles.
- Facilitating the women to fully utilize their potential and develop professional orientation at work place.

b) Profile of participants:
Barring Spring board programmes, the participants were women officers, drawn from Marketing, R&P, R&D Center. They represented CO, HOS, units and regions and were a mix of grades from A to E.

c) Identification of the following themes for designing the training programme were:

- Career development and growth perspectives.
- Professionalization at work place.
- Mobility across organization
- Balancing multiple roles in harmony
- Self-Development
- Stereotypes and interface with the emerging scenario.

As a training strategy, the belief was that in order to get optimal results, the design, inputs, and delivery of the programmes were extremely important and had to be done in consultation with an expert woman faculty who had conducted studies in the area of women and was well familiar with cultural, social and psychological dimension of womens life. The training programmes were to be held both at Divisional as well as the Corporate level. The following programmes were conducted:

- Career Development Strategies
- Career Development Perspectives
- Partnership and Inter Dependence
- Life goal planning workshop
- Managerial Role profile workshop
- Spring board training
- Assertiveness skills workshop.

Study on career of women in the context of work, family, organization, self and society was done by post graduate student trainee from department of applied psychology, Delhi university , the summary of findings of which are presented below:

At the work front, a majority of women had a positive attitude, and found it to be a source of maximum satisfaction. They showed an interest in adopting to advanced technology and undergo training to improve their skills at work. But approximately one-third of the women population felt that they lacked assertiveness and confidence in their capabilities which hampered their career growth. A sizeable portion of these women denied themselves the opportunity of growth and development due to insecurity and lack of confidence.

Apart from this, a majority of them seemed to be able to draw a demarcation between family problems and job demands. At the family front a working status helped a woman to provide additional money to her family which increased her status in the family. A very high majority of women spent considerable amount of time in performing family duties and more than half of them denied themselves opportunities for career development due to family compulsions. More than three-fourths of the total number of women shared that their husbands felt proud of their professional achievements and they showed lot of trust and confidence with their spouse.

At the level of the organisation it seemed that the company had been able to give its employees a comfortable and encouraging environment at large. Still, the high achievers did not appear to be satisfied with their growth opportunities. By growth opportunities it meant training, promotions and perks and challenging work assignments. Gender based discrimination existed in the organization. There were also remote cases of sexual harassment.

The company understood the responsibilities women had towards their family and made the required adjustments. But a small portion of the population felt that more flexibility could be allowed. Approximately one-third of the women population of this organization was not clear of the rules and regulations relating to their working conditions.

But overall a very high majority of women were working due to their own desire to work. They felt that work gave them a distinct identity and a sense of autonomy and power. Three-fourths of of the total number of women felt that they were less ambitious than men and they had 'extra' qualities to contribute to the success of the organisation. The responses indicated that these women had been able to build a 'work-identity'. But more than half of the population felt that getting involved in their career had introduced a new role into their lives which interfered with their role of a mother and a wife.

At the level of the society there had been an improvement in the status of Indian women in the nineties. They received support and encouragement from friends, relatives and significant other people. Society had also started accepting working women. Still, the status of women in India needed to be improved further. A large number of women felt that they were getting equal recognition as their husband at home and outside, but still a sizeable number of women felt that they were not being considered equal to the men at home or outside.

d) Content of Training for trainer's programme:

For the purpose of the programme the six modules designed were as follows:

(a) Life Space analysis (b) Life Role analysis (c) Systems analysis (d) Interface analysis and (e) Skill Building

Life space and life role analysis gets anchored and integrated in the analysis of the managerial role. Two instruments – Managerial Role Matrix and Adjectival Analysis Psychogram would provide the primary structural setting for generation data. The setting for processing this data would be semi-structured. The processing would build the links of managerial role taking processes and the psychological role stance with the cultural identities.

A decade or more of women entering and persisting in the diverse field of management has established an irreversible momentum and they have come to be part of organizations and management. The fact that women are late entrants in organizations and specifically in managerial roles raised many issues. Did women need training in management? Or like the initial phenomenon of industrial development the traditional assumptions operated that once on the job and in the role stance women would learn and do what the jobs and organization require them to do. The second issue linked to the first is whether training need be given to women in groups of women or women be part and parcel of training being given to any employee in the organization be they women or men?

The participants in the workshop explored the above issue at length. Based on the cross cultural and diverse experiences of the participants the experience was that women needed training not only in management but also on specific issues of being women in management as managers. The rationale being that on the job training and their managerial role performance may make them functionally trained but women also carry with them the additional dimension of home and work interface which is unique to women. It has been debated that men also carry the dimension of home and work. However, their dilemma is allocation of time rather than grappling with multiple roles and systems as traditionally prescribed by the society. All societies across the world legitimise men's dominant transactions with the environment and as such the external interface. While societies across the world legitimise women's internal interface with home and children. Women's entry into the world of organization and managerial role confronts them with the struggle to feel legitimate and simultaneously manage the two inerfaces of external and internal environment. As such, it was felt that until such a time that a critical mass of women are trained and that a critical mass of organizations and employers are sensitized to the entry and position of women in organization it was necessary that specific focus on training women in management be retained.

The focus of management training is to empower women take active and participative role in policies, influence strategies and be part of structure. How does a women make a departure in her role taking anchored in social structure and processes of the culture? The experience of third world representatives suggested that in order to bring about enduring capabilities in individuals, to make new responses, inputs are necessary first to evolve new dimensions of organizations, structures, systems, tasks and their roles in it. In the absence of such a grounding all inputs remain at cognitive level and do not empower individuals to make new responses, discover new meanings for their role taking and new action choices.

Figure 2 reflects how identity is anchored both in emotive and cognitive maps of roles and systems.

The discussions during the workshops have reflected that once, women can explore the issues of themselves, of their self image, their concept of space and its legitimacy in both social and work settings and learn to give value to themselves, they can make departures from their role archored in social structure.

Figure 4
Structures Systems and Environment and Role taking processes

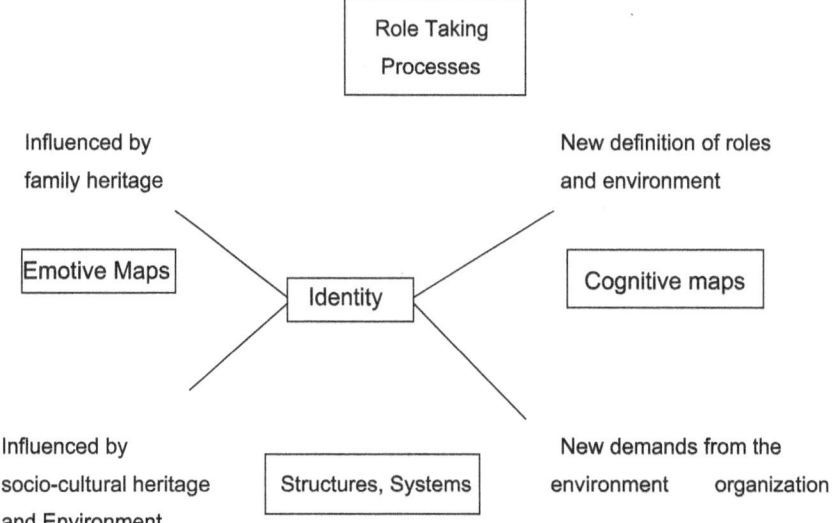

- Values
- Beliefs
- Attitudes
- Attitude and skills learnt could be translated into relevant and meaningful action choices.

- Many women managers have learnt a lot from many training programmes. When they return home to their work settings and confront barriers, the awareness through training makes them perceive the organisation as a place which blocks their growth.
- Learning then is either ignored or considered not applicable or possible to implement in their organization.

What perhaps is necessary to explore is the way the concept of relevant and appropriate technology became significant , similarly the concept of training also needs to discover relevant and appropriate management systems.

Creation of Small groups:

The creation of small groups in this experiential approach were spaces where a set of participants came together to explore specific experiences and issues which they had with themselves. Here in these groups individuals could explore what was the nature of the socio-psychological world they lived in, what were their experiences, what meanings they gave to people and situations, what feelings they experienced and what barriers and inhibitions they held. In essence, the invitation was to pause, reflect and articulate what each individual did in moments of stress, when alone. Specifically, the objectives of the small group were to invite the participants to:

- Share with each other the experiences of living in the world of family, work and community.
- To share the pressures and demands of multiple roles and multiple systems and discover the facilitating and inhibiting processes within them.
- To explore the nature of familial and formal role relationships and the nature and quality of inter-personal transactions.
- To explore the stereotypes of men and women that they held and the implications of those to the emergence of working relationships in formal work settings.

- To explore the experiences of both familial and organisational authority so as to discover new ways of relating to authority.
- To make a realistic appraisal of one's strengths and limitations and to design an actor role for the self.
- To explore the definitions and meanings of family and work structures, affiliative and task relationships, personal and impersonal authority and the quality of role taking both in the family and the organisation.
- To explore the nature of membership in the collectively, institution and system and to explore the interfaces of the self with the collectively, institution, culture, society, family organisation and environment.

Small groups were settings where sharing and exploration became easier. Cumulative stresses could be stated and there was an invitation to listen. The experiences of small groups had reflected specific themes and patterns for women and men.

C) The Various Workshops:

A) Strategies for career development of women:
The objectives of the workshop were to:

- Help participants appreciate the objectives, structure and goals of Women in Public Sector (WIPS).
- Examine the organizational (IOC's) perspective and development policies for women.
- Facilitate exploration of the needs, opportunities and constraints of women employees in their multiple roles and propose strategies for their optimal development.

The programme enabled the participants to undertake the following:

- Identification of opportunities and constraints that women generally experienced at three crucial stages in their work career i.e. (a) early career, (b) mid career and (c) late career.

- Exploration of the psychological dimensions of the women's role, its linkages with folk lore and culture, and how some of these dimensions needed to be reoriented in order that women were fully integrated into business systems and structures.

B) Career development perspectives for women:

As a fall out of the earlier workshop it became apparent that women managers needed to develop an appreciation of the critical role of 'Mobility' in the enrichment of & advancement of careers. At the same time the marketing division around this time was experiencing the constraints of concentration of women officers in the Host Regions. There was need felt for women to move from job & career orientation to professionalism. Considering all these urgent demands, it was decided to design a typical programme for the benefit of marketing division which would enable the women to under stand and consider the issue of mobility favourably.

Workshop's Objectives were to:

- Enable the woman executives gain insights into their social and organizational context and their role in it.
- To understand organisational realities and business and task objectives in the context of the changing environment.
- Explore strategies for integrating women in their multiple roles for their optimal development and enhanced contribution.
- Redefine and redesign for professionalisation of their role and management.

C) Exploring partnership & Inter-dependence in professional roles:

Workshop Objectives were:

- To explore the issue of women's entry and as such gender issues in the organisations.
- To explore the maps and definitions held by men and women managers about the organisation and each other.

- To explore superior – subordinate and colleague interface with specific focus on men superiors and women subordinates and vice-versa.
- To identify social, cultural and professional forces impacting and influencing both men and women managers
- To arrive at a shared understanding of the new roles required for being professional men and women in organisation.

D) Life Goal Planning Workshop for Women Executives:

Workshop Objectives were:
- Explore women's concept of job, career and profession.
- Explore issues of system, structure, authority and managerial roles.
- Explore women's issues in life space and life role to arrive at professional roles in torganisation.
- Enable women to accept self and value of themselves for effectiveness at work and wholesomeness in their social system.

E) Managerial Role Profile for Women Executives:

Workshop Objectives were:
- Find out about the Managerial Role Profile of – Women Managers
- Establish an identity
- Explore how we attribute meanings to managerial processes
- Resolve dilemma of social and professional roles to integrate into professional Approach.

F) Assertiveness Skills for Women Managers:

Workshop Objectives were:
- To enable women managers to become more effective through their understanding and practice of assertiveness skills.
- To apply assertiveness to practical management from the workplace.
- To enhance managerial effectiveness through the use of assertiveness.
- To produce personal action plans

D) Future Directions:

There was an urgent need felt for women to move from social structures, roles and processes to work structures, roles and processes. It is not an either/or choice but an added new concept and dimension of professional role taking. In this transition work becomes a significant part of life space. Tasks and performance acquire efficiency, effectiveness, and new meaning. Both become essential criteria for professionalism. Women also need to give themselves legitimacy in formal planning, policy formulation and strategic choices. They need to acquire a competitive edge and professional parity by acquiring knowledge, attitudes and skills anchored in a personal / professional perspective.

For women, it was breaking a new path. It was an uphill struggle. However, if women found freedom to accept their legitimacy in new contexts by investing in their own learning and growth, the chances were they would experience success and achievement. They would also find others in both new roles, and provide support to others. Tomorrow's institutions would be confronted with new challengers. If responsiveness to these by both women and men was a response by default, then women primarily will fall by the wayside and would deprive themselves of opportunities of growth. It was essential that women take charge of their own destiny and gave shape to substantive roles in the system.

Essentially, all these designs explored how women shaped their roles and defined their membership in the respective systems. The women had to question their socio-cultural beliefs, their own need to hold on to structured normative prescriptions, and realistically assess their strengths and limitations. Women had to create new spaces, meaningful relationships in the family and work with women and men. Essentially, the effort was to experience success by achieving fulfillment in tasks and relationships.

Women and Leadership Roles: Past and Present

Introduction

The Human Journey has witnessed 5000 years of civilisation. In this journey a great mass of cultural heritage and cultural baggage of the past is cumulatively carried by society and its people. Culture generally reflects the myths, epics, folklores, folktales land all other sagas of men and women who are epitomised as heroes and villians and gets carried as a cultural coding of life. The role models adopted by men and women in that specific time and era are also carried, which over time are idealised and which influence the shaping of the nature of relationships, and interfaces across roles. This in turn determines the roles to be taken by women and men. These relationships can be in the form of a wide variety of social roles and relationships, man-woman relationships and parenting. Social roles are governed by social structures (i.e. traditions in terms of events in which men, women, societies, systems come together) and social processes related to roles that men and women take in society. The cultural heritage includes the positive role models which provide us directions to lead life. Similarly, the cultural baggage of the past inhibits both women and men to take new initiatives, make departures, redefine and redesign newer roles and processes and also contributes to entrenchment in the past and also obsolete role models. Any understanding of Indian women, of their identity, and especially of their inner dialogue, will be incomplete without a walk down the corridors of Indian history where women have paused, lived and internalised various role models. Some have taken leadership roles while millions of others have taken the role of victims. The role of Indian women, as it has evolved, been experienced and understood over 4,000 years, has been intertwined with the history of the country which is primarily one of repeated impositions of an alien ethos on its culture necessiating a frequent restructuring of social systems and consequently, individual identity. The role of Indian women has ranged from that of a deity to that of a devdasi, from being pure to being vulgar, from being supreme to being downtrodden, and also as innumerable manifestations of virtue or vice.

The woman evokes in man a range of emotions. She evokes lust and passion as well as devotion, she promises union, and physical fulfilment as well as communion; and at all times she arouses anxiety, apprehensions and fears. She goes by several names. Sometimes she is called a goddess, sometimes Shakti and often a witch who is both seductive and fickle. She is the temptress and the rejuvenator.

Presented below are five Archetype Role Models of ancient India.

Kannagi, Sita, Savitri, Draupadi representing mythological role models and Rani Ki Jhansi in the historical context. All these women depict having qualities of strength, will power and faith and confidence in themselves. Their love and sacrifice for husband and families is indicative in the stories presented below:

1) Kannagi

The Story of **Kannagi**, the central heroine of the Epic of the story goes thus. Kannagi and her husband Kovalan, while on their way to

Madurai from Poompuhar come across a tribal group where tribal goddess speaking from the shamaness declared Kannagi to be the queen of all Tamil Lands. It was hard at that time to understand that, not realising what fate really had in store for them. Upon reaching Madurai, Kovalan tried to sell one of Kannagi's bracelet. Coincidently, the queen's identical looking bracelets were stolen and court goldsmith without realising that the two brackets were different (i.e., rubies were embedded within Kovalan's anklet and pearls were present within the queen's anklet) declared Kovalan guilty and the king's court put him to death. Kannagi was filled with rage upon hearing the news and rushed to the court and proved her point. Upon hearing this, the king died of his own volition. Kannagi was filled with utmost rage and fury and cut off one of her breasts and threw it against the city's walls which caught fire. According to beliefs, the god of fire – Agni could have done this for her. In the process, many evil people died and the animals and good people remained. Some of them followed Kannagi as they believed her to be a goddess. Kannagi, then ascended to heaven and united with her husband. The strength Kannagi had within is imperative from the fact that even after seeing her husband on death bed she ran to the King's court to prove him non-guilty of the charge put against him.

2) Sita

Sita in the Valmiki Ramayana is not exactly representative for Vedic Stridharma.

To begin with, she chooses her own husband in a competitive swayamvara-'only the strongest and the smartest prince will do'. Again, after Kaikeyi's intervention, when Ram goes into forest exile, she insists on accompanying him. Sita's strength and self-possession are apparent. She is dutiful, indeed, but she has to argue her case in order to do what she knows is right. She is not an obedient servant to a godlike husband; she has a will of her own and her relationship to Rama is governed by love for him, rather than obedience to his orders. She shows her determination and independence throughout the years in the forest; her insistence that Rama got the gold-spotted deer and her command that Lakshman comes to his rescue, eventually leads to her abduction by Ravana. She shows self-control and she does not give in to Ravana's will. On being freed, she defends herself whole-heartedly against Rama's accusations. She is far from passive. It is in the context of this "dwelling in another man's house", that Vedic regulations for women are invoked and popular sentiment demands an ordeal to prove her purity. This strength of character has not gone unnoticed by Indian women, who have found much in her to applaud. Despite being commonly held up as a paragon of the submissiveness, obedience, and loyalty that many men would like to see in their wives, women have often taken other lessons from her behaviour. To many Hindu women, she is a great heroine, not just a goddess. Sita is a unique ideal of fidelity and chastity. She had to undergo unbearable trial and tribulations throughout her life but with the power of her unshakable fidelity and dedication to her husband she bore all the difficulties of life with fortitude. She along with her husband, smilingly enjoyed the hardships of life in jungle. The rakshasa, king Ravana failed to lower her morale or weaken her moral strength. It was through the ordeal of fire that Sita proved and established her virtue and stainlessness of her character. With the injury of the time of exile, (Vanavasa) Sri Rama in order to satisfy some of his subjects, banished Sita who remained in the hermitage of Rishi Valmiki. The very fact that Rama and Sita are always mentioned in one breath endows Sita with equality: whatever status Rama occupies this will also be Sita's. If he is king, she will be queen, if he is god, she will become his goddess. However, she is queen and goddess on her own merit, not because of Rama's grace.

3) Savitri

Savitri who is mentioned among great chaste and faithful godly women, took Satyavan as her husband knowing fully well that he would not live long. When only four days of his age were remaining she undertook a vow to defeat death. On the fourth day Satyavan died with Yamaraja (The god of death) walking away with his vitality. Savitri walked pursuing Yamaraja. As they were walking one behind the other, on the way there occurred a "question-answer" between them. Yamaraja was very much impressed by the gentle behaviour of Savitri, her wisdom, her one pointed devotion (dedication) to her husband. Getting pleased he asked Savitri to ask for boons. Savitri asked for such boons which not only obtain for her the well-being of both her father's and her husband's families but Yamaraja had also to return the vitality of Satyavana. Savitri with the power of her chastity and fidelity protected her good fortune.

4) Draupadi

Draupadi was a very impressive and brilliant and strong personality (character) in Mahabharata. The daughter of Drupada, the king of Panchala (Punjab), came to Hastinapur as a daughter-in-law of the Kuru-clan on being won by Arjuna, at her Swayamvara, by piercing with arrow the eye of a moving fish on a high pole, looking in to the fish's image in a cauldron of oil below. She was never ready to compromise on either her rights as a daughter-in-law or even on the rights of the Pandavas and remained ever ready to fight back or avenge high-handedness and injustice meted out to her and them. Draupadi had absolute faith in Sri Krishna. She was also dear to Sri Krishna equal to his real sister. Draupadi put through much suffering and disgrace in life. Dussasana tried to remove her clothes and as such made an attempt to violate her modesty in full view of the assembly. During the days of the banishment to jungle of the Pandavas, Jayadratha made an attempt to abduct her during the period of their dwelling secretly. Keechaka wanted to outrage her modesty. After the duration of their stay in the jungle was over, Draupadi, with a view to fulfill her vow (promise to herself to tie her untied hair after washing them with the blood of Dussasana) and to punish all those who had disgraced her and perpetrated offence against her, blazed the fire of revenge burning in her heart into the hearts and minds of Pandayas. The refulgence (glow) of

Draupadi's lustrous prototype of womanhood shall always be a source of inspiration for the women of India.

5) Queen of Jhansi – Lakshmi Bai

Lakshmi Bai, the Rani of Jhansi in northern India, led an uprising against a takeover of the homeland by the British. She became a heroine and a symbol of resistance to the British rule. When Rani Lakshmi Bai rose against the British in 1857 AD she immortalized Jhansi. She has since become a heroine of the Indian independence movement, a sort of central Indian Joan of Arc. Lakshmi Bai was born around 1830 into a wealthy, high caste Brahmin family. She was named Manukarnika, which is one of the names of the holy river Ganges. As a young woman she learned to read, write and debate. She also learned to ride horses and use weapons while playing with her adopted brothers. She accepted the name Lakshmi Bai when she married Gangadhar Rao, the Maharajah of Jhansi and became the Rani, (short for Maharani, the wife of Maharajah) of Jhansi. Gangadhar Rao was between forty and fifty years of age at the time of their wedding. This was his second marriage. His first wife died without producing an heir. The new Rani of Jhansi gave birth to a son, but he died when he was three months old. Subsequently, Damodar Rao, Gangadhar's relative, became their adopted son. In 1853, Gangadhar Rao died. The Governor-General of India, the Marquess of Dalhousie, announced that since Gangadhar Rao left no heir, the state of Jhansi would be annexed by the British Government. The British rejected the claim that Damodar Rao was the legal heir. According to Hindu law, little Damodar Rao was Gangadhar's heir and successor. In the Hindu religion, a surviving son, either biological or adopted, had an obligation to perform certain sacrifices after his father's death to prevent his father from being condemned to punishment inhell. The refusal of the British to acknowledge the legitimacy of Rajah's adopted son caused a serious consternation in the local population. Rani appealed her case to London, but that appeal was turned down. Not wishing to give up her kingdom, Lakshmi Bai assembled a volunteer army of 14,000 rebels and ordered that defenses of the city itself be strengthened. Jhansi was attacked by the British in March 1858. Shelling of Jhansi was fierce and the British were determined not to allow any rebels to escape while Rani was determined not to surrender. The British noted that the Indian soldiers fighting them showed more vigor than they ever had while following British orders. Women were also seen working like batteries and carrying ammunition, food and water to the soldiers. Rani, herself, was seen constantly active in the defense of the city. Jhansi, however, fell to the British forces after a two-week srege. She, however managed to escape on horseback under the cover of darkness and within twenty-four hours rode over one hundred miles to the fortress of Kalpi. Several other Indian rulers joined the rebel forces there. It is believed that Rani was influential in convincing the others to go on the offensive and seize the fortress of Gwalior. This manoeuver was successful and helped rally by the rebel forces together. It was not long, however, before the British forces determined to win Gwalior back. A fierce battle ensued. Rani was in charge of the eastern side of defense, however, she lost her life on the second day of fighting. The British won back Gwalior. Rani's body was given a ceremonial cremation and burial by the faithful servants. Sir Hugh Rose, the commander of the British force, wrote later "The Rani was remarkable for her bravery, cleverness and perseverance; her generosity to her subordinates was unbounded. These qualities, combined with her rank, rendered her the most dangerous of all the rebel leaders". A popular Indian ballad said:

How valiantly like a man fought she,

The Rani of Jhansi

On every parapet a gun she set

Raining fire to hell,

How well like a man fought the Rani of Jhansi

How valiantly and well.

As we set ourselves first to explore the role models available from the cultural lore and mythological figure as depicted in the above, we then examined what alternatives are available to Indian women that enable them to reach the psychological threshold with which to create a wholesome world for themselves. We discovered that there are five basic themes in our cultural lore around which Indian Women build their roles and crystallize their destiny.

Organizations which design career paths for their female employees face issues of promotion, appraisal, competition between men and women colleagues, stereotypes about women in leadership roles and positions, and the personality traits of women leaders. Research findings (Parikh I.J 1990, Parikh I.J and Shah. N 1992, Parikh I.J 1998, Parikh I.J and Engineer M.F 1999) suggest that women are capable and competent, are effective decision makers and can exercise authority. They take significant responsibilities in organizations and aspire for positions that are appropriate to the tasks they are doing. More and more women who opt for careers make hard choices, strive for performance and achievement and finally succeed in reaching senior positions.

During an address on February 25, 1998 at the inaugural event in a lecture series on Leadership, the President of Penn State University shared her thoughts and experiences about competitiveness and leadership:

- Success should not be measured in terms of polarities. The label-'success' or 'failure' has an impact on self-definition. Self-definition or Self-fulfillment could be sought by cherishing and searching for complexities, embracing ambiguities, taking risks and rejecting polarities.
- Leadership roles emerge when one follows the heart by doing what one loves. Passion and vision are the hallmarks of leadership.
- Women are gifted with the skills that they can develop as professional strengths to become effective leaders. The ability to bring people together, to encourage dialogue, build consensus and most importantly understand the social and emotional needs of others – all these qualities can bring about

a significant change in the organization as all these are effective qualities needed to be a leader.

- Competitiveness is a quality essential for great leadership and many women tend to shy away from it. Healthy competition leads to internalized goal-setting and less fear of success. The willingness to share ideas, take risks, acquire new skills, forge new relationships and share feelings can go a long way in creating an environment which develops leadership qualities in women.

- When a woman raises child, she understands and learns about herself. The child rearing expands the definitions of success and commitment to leadership, as it becomes a challenge for the parent to make the world a better place for his young one. It is a challenge for mothers of today's generation to offer to their children, especially a male child, the opportunity to see the gender gap closing. The children of tomorrow stand for a generation which is shaped by the changing roles, concerns and problems of women and men, where there is more equality at work and at home. A healthier and happier society will emerge if there is involvement of men in supporting their spouse's career and in parenting of children. It would also help evolve more women to assume leadership roles.

The role of Indian women has undergone dramatic and drastic changes from era to era, while within the eras themselves there have existed simultaneous contradictions. This in itself has created problems for contemporary women in experiencing a continuity of thier identity with society. What is introjected by a woman growing up in Indian society is perhaps a collage and a flux of attitudes, perceptions, roles and locations of their identity. It seems to be difficult to take a logical look at all this. To every "yes" there is a "no" and to every "no" there is a "yes". The introjected collage does not, therefore, make it easy for women to define their role and take leadership roles and to enunciate directions and goals for themselves. (Parikh, Indira. J., Garg, Pulin. K., 1989) It would be better understood if one looks at the historical perspectives given below:

A historical perspective:

This can be divided into:

    a)   The evolution of women in terms of the attitudes/beliefs they carry , their role-taking and finally deriving meanings in life through career and growth, and also the change of concept of the society from the agrarian era to the present day.

    b)   The thresholds of growth of women from birth to adulthood

a) The evolution of women from the agrarian beliefs to the 90's:

1) Beginning – First steps from the family:

Social beliefs / Categories of Role Taking by men and women in the society were reflective of the attitudes / beliefs which were operative when men / women encountered each other in organization. All these codings were from the society. However, newer voices with newer meanings were beginning to emerge. Women in senior positions and in leadership roles were going beyond the male models of leadership and emerging with their own branch of leadership

2) First experiences – from education:

Personal meaning of role came forth . In agrarian society women had always been

    working. The equation earlier however was that age and experience would be equivalent to knowledge and wisdom. In educational institutions , the concept changed to having education, career and fresh minds equivalent to more information and more oppurtunities. The concept of hierarchy has become topsy-turvy.

3) Entry into Work – Crossed threshold:

Crossing of a very major threshold in terms of making departures from, what the social codings, family etc, would say, emerged. The women who entered the work set ups in 60's, 70's 80's 90;s – there was a distinct shift but underlying processes had not dramatically changed.

4) Settling down – Two kinds of experiences were being perceived– from entry to work, to acceptance for work, to absorption to work:

In terms of passage of time this movement was turbulent – a test of fire. If this was legitimised one would be prepared. But unfortunately organizations do not prepare men/women. The men carry the maps and definitions from the social structures, Therefore a lot of hostility, resentment between men and women in organization is experienced. The controversy that "If women claim to be equal why do they want more privileges", prevails throughout organisations.

5) Present Dilemmas – 90's changing the world upside down:

The kind of opportunities available, especially technology has made easy for women to work at home. But today the concept of work for majority of women is seen as income generation and to improve the quality of life and living. For many it is a career and for a very few it has become a professional role which they need to give meaning to themselves. Women have to interface with superiors, colleagues and subordinates, where the combinations are-superior as male, subordinate as female ; superior as female, subordinate as male ; or male and female as colleagues,– where there can be unmarried man and married woman ; married man and unmarried woman or both married or unmarried. Each of these dimensions contribute to a working relationship.

b) Thresholds of growth of women from birth to adulthood:

Let us examine the Pattern of Evolution:

1. Birth to Infancy:

This determines the emotional responsiveness. Residues of what it means to be a female child are carried, swallowing everything especially the messages which are conveyed experientially.

2 . Infancy to childhood:

Education /institutions, give shape to re-inforce what we have absorbed from the family. What kind of psychological role will we play and live with? is determined in this stage.

3 . Childhood to Adolescence:

This is a stage where encounter between male and female is experienced.

What kind of conceptualisation do we have about relationships? comes forth during this stage.

4 . Adolescence to Adulthood:

Entering our own life-space,is what one experiences here. After which patterns follow, -unfolding of marriage / enduring relationships / parenting, is experienced.

For centuries women lived the myth of no location and no space for themselves, shame of their body, of being born a girl child, marginalised in the institutions of family and denied access to basic dignity of health, hygiene, decent living conditions and/or growth oppurtunities. The women were denied, deprived, discriminated and were then idealised and glorified in their victimhood, martyrdom and surrendering of their own identity. The men lived the myth of providers, and as such the were regarded as owners, brave and strong to protect the women and children. Significance, centrality, the power and authority and providing direction were the domain of men. In this century however women have travelled a long distance. The journey has been arduous and uphill. The effort to push the women downhill into the abyss of middle ages and Victorian era have been many. The might and power of this effort has had the reinforcement of centuries old traditions embedded in the role definitions of women and men in the society. However, the women of this century have discovered the Herculean spirit of persistence, the phoenix like quality of resilience and an ability to grasp the straws of education, to have career options and to unfold their lives in a manner different from their mothers and grandmothers. The women have struggled to walk side by side with men and catch up the distance of centuries with the rest of their counterparts in the society. The effort is to give shape to a more human, dignified relatedness between the two-the man and the woman, the girl child and the boy child and the collectivity of women and men. (Parikh, Indira. J., WP.No.98-05-02, May, 1998). In this process women have entered the portals of work and organisations and have taken up leadership roles.

Experiences of Organizational Transformation By Women in Leaderships Roles:

The women shared their lives and experiences of growing up as well as their experiences in the organisation. The observations were:

- Women have entered various new professions which are not traditional like, teaching, nursing etc., Earlier women entered work not out of choice but due to economic reasons or some calamity befalling them and their family.

- Women's entry into formal work organisations has been a decade later then men. Women, like men carried social, cultural and personal maps from their traditional roles to the work places.

- Women are performing dual roles where priority needs to be given to the home-front as it is the women who manage the household. Although many felt that times are changing as increasingly the husband's role is supportive to both women and home. However, women continue to carry feelings of guilt when it comes to their interface with children and anger when it comes to their interface with in-laws. The social-coding and the cultural-coding, eventually becomes a personal coding resulting in dilemmas of marriage around relationships and specially motherhood.

- Women end up taking up more and more responsibilities at work and often work for 16 hours a day. However women take a step backward in taking leadership roles and positions. Not many have broken through the senior management cadre to reach the higher echlons of management.

- Increasingly there is a change of attitude amongst men in perceiving women who are working (Parikh, Indira J, November 1989). Earlier, if a women was successful the assumption was "somebody else e.g a man was behind her success". There was invariably a postulation of a godfather. If a women was friendly with a male colleague – it was always felt that she was having an affair. Platonic relationships were deemed to be improbable. However, many women felt that there is definitely a shift in these perceptions. Today if a women is succeeding it is perceived that she is hardworking and she has earned the position. Women experience a constant pressure to perform and prove themselves in their work place. They face a constant challenge to achieve and prove themselves that they are capable, competent and deserve the promotion and the position.

- The women at work experienced that the women peers were not supportive of women whereas their male counterparts accepted them and were more supportive.

- In a hard core male dominated society, women continue to deal with personal stereotypes and remarks around clothes, dressing and attire. "Silly questions" are asked in interviews which are generally aimed to dissuade women from taking the up the job or push her to guage her resillience or dislocate her from her confidence. Women have learnt to survive and face the reality as a challenge. Women have learnt to deal with such situations logically and rationally or by being nonchalant under these circumstances.

- Women are perceived and related with differently than their male colleagues at the work place. If women present themselves as weak and mild, they are exploited. If they are assertive they are perceived as aggressive.

- The aggressiveness is reflected in women acquiring strong opinions, getting entrenched in arguments, loosing flexibility and negotiability, insensitivity to others opinions and feelings, becoming closed, loosing openness and empathy and overall acquiring an attitude of "I know better" (Parikh Indira .J, W.P.no. 98-05-02, 1998).

- Some women shared that at higher levels there are generally men who occupy the significant positions. Women are fewer and far apart. Women experience discrimination in processes leading to promotion. Often the organization policies are different for male and female employees. For eg. in one of the organisation the policy of medical reimbursement for dependents favoured men. Men could claim medical expenses for their parents but a women could not do so for her in-laws or her parents. However, there are changes in the organisation where some women shared that they did not face any such gender bias in their organizational policies.

- Most women believed that there is a shift in mindset of how women are experienced in the organziations. More and more men are accepting that women are competent, intelligent and capable. Women can generate resources. In some profession, women are even considered better than men and in some organizations women are appreciated in terms of being hard working and also in terms of the values and beliefs they carry. The earlier myths which perpetuated in the organization that women's success has a sexual connotation or an impression that women's success is due to a god-father is definitely being replaced by women being regarded as competent, capable, hardworking and committed. Many women felt that though these are the first healthy signs, a large multitude of women still continue to live with stereotype images and expectations of women.

Assumptions of Society in Agrarian Era

Across the world the human civilisation went through a long period of agrarian beginning and consolidation in the social structures, processes and roles. The agrarian society in India can be traced back to about 2500 years. Today, India is a multi-diverse and multi-cultural nation and the society and people from rural and urban reality continue to have distinctiveness and uniqueness. The agrarian society operated with some basic assumptions. These assumptions then defined women and men's desirable roles in societies. The shift of Indian society from agrarian to industrial and rural to urban is characterised by the following distinct features, which in turn shaped women and men's roles:

- The agrarian society clearly defined the roles of men and women. Men interfaced with the external environment while women interfaced with the internal environment of home, family and relationships.
- Social living and work were quite integrated in the agricultural social design through caste and community affiliations. The integrated life of social and work revolved around the seasons of nature. Events of social institutions like marriage, birth, death and festivals created and brought communities together or resulted in conflict.
- Men worked alone – women lived in groups / communities. Communities got together to give an expression to their togetherness. As industrialisation took place and external influences impacted the society, the above assumptions began to change. With the set-up of formal work organizations, women like men, got educated, interfaced with the external environment, left home and started working. The women began equipping themselves with occupational expertise. For

the first time men and women in organizations encountered each other without their social roles / baggages, but with their competencies and capabilities. Initially most found it difficult to relate with each other. Moreover as more women entered and continued working, the acceptance of the fact that women can also contribute equally at work, began to emerge.

- Society / organization and families therefore encountered many new interfaces. For e.g. as contrast to the agrarian society where men worked alone, men in organizations are required to work in groups and the concept of team-work has acquired immense significance. In contrast to the earlier context where women lived in groups, in urban centres she lives alone. However, the wherewithal's of managing the external interface of the environment as well as managing relationships at home creates stress for women.

- For women in society, meaning in life has largely come from relationships, and for men it has also come from being a good son to his family.

Thus centuries of the agrarian ethos fostered values and attitudes, patterns of interpersonal relationships and meanings of life which became deeply embedded in the psyche of the culture and society. In fact, they became so absolute that they were assumed to be a part of the basic nature of human beings. The concepts of life, predisposition to action, and curtailed aspirations to which individuals adapted themselves came to be treated either as being God-given or as being essentially inherent qualities of human beings. Thus, individuals became the victims of their own natural, social and spiritual adaptations, which societies call heritage. With the emergence of the industrial era, which coincided with the independence of the country, a whole new process of work ethics, technology and, consequently, a new life-style got introduced. According to Parikh and Garg, girls in large numbers joined schools and colleges. For the first time, they glimpsed a world which was earlier the exclusive domain of men. A whole new vista opened up before the

Indian woman. She discovered she could do well in her studies; that her intelligence was hers to shape and enhance. She discovered the magic of choices, options and alternatives. Women entered the portals of medicine, engineering, administrative services, politics, law, teaching, and the mushrooming business organizations and manufacturing industries. Slowly but steadily, they moved into skilled and semi-skilled jobs, and a small number even succeeded in joining what were considered 'elite' professions . Through education, women from the better off socio-economic strata became aware of the existing social disparities and of the condition of women in general, particularly of those belonging to socially and economically deprived groups. Some of these women joined clubs like the Lions to participate in voluntary social programs for the socially and economically deprived. It soon became a status symbol to join these organizations, to be involved in fund-raising or charitable activities, and be considered part of the emancipated or "avant-garde" lot. Parents of educated girls also recognised their high economic potential. To them, their daughter's economic self-reliance was an asset in marriage and could, hopefully, lead to a reduction in the dowry demanded. Economic independence also served as an insurance against future uncertainties, and only education could provide opportunities for this independence. However, caught between the conflicting demands of achievement as both an instrument of autonomy and of insurance, many of these women became highly ambivalent. At one level, they welcomed the opportunities for enhancement and growth but, at another level, found that these opportunities did not provide them with the desired self-worth and respect. It became extremely difficult for these women to value themselves and their existence; the insecurity of their relationships filled them with guilt, anxiety, anger and resentment, and a sense of helplessness at being considered a burden in the community (Parikh, Indira. J., and Garg, Pulink. K., 1989).

As such, all the process of cultural, social and familial socialisation anchored in the agrarian model of living and relationship came into direct confrontation with the experiences, expectations and aspirations of today's role requirements of women. This century and specifically in the last five decades women have made significant shifts in their location in the social structure, in their role taking in family settings and the external environment. One such significant shift has been their transition from homes to that of formal work organizations and their role taking from social Affiliative relations to managerial roles (Parikh, Indira. J., W.P.No.941, June 1991).

Women's Life Space

Many women have struggled with the system which has often attempted to deploy their potentials both at home and in the work setting. They have often confronted within themselves the pathos of the traditional past and the aspired ethos of the present times, but in doing so has overloaded themselves with the processes of both. Most of them have sustained themselves by over-engaging in both roles. Others have fallen either into the role of a daughter, or a wife, or a mother. Thus, they have found it difficult to evolve an integrated identity. (Parikh, Indira. J., and Garg, Pulink. K., 1989).

Although the Indian family setting provides eventual support to women working in organizations it also creates tremendous guilt and stress. Each new step the woman takes she is shown the prescriptive social ideal role model of an ever sacrificing woman – a victim and a martyr. Her own ambition, achievement, involvement in work generates threats and anxieties in the significant role holders of the family, viz., the husband, the in-laws and the children. The husband puts her in the middle of two systems and questions her loyalty to the family setting. The in-laws demand the traditional ideal role model of a daughter-in-law; and the children demand her presence at all times. Indian women executes in the name of exclusive responsibility of a dual career and belonging in two systems, gets pulled and pushed between two competing systems, multiple roles and expectations (Parikh, Indira. J., & Shah, Nayana. A., W.P.No.941, June, 1991)

Dilemmas of Marriage:

The socialisation process to shape women's role as a daughter, daughter-in-law, wife and mother is rooted in the social and cultural codlings of the past. What becomes apparent is that though women are aware of the cultural codlings, woman after woman continue to seek acceptance, affirmation and recognition as a good and acceptable daughter-in-law by surrendering to role conformity. Many voiced the anguish that their experience of the role of daughter-in-law and sister-in-law was that they were largely seen as an intruder, and an outsider, who took away the son or the brother. Even when the mother had a significant role in the selection of the person as the bride for the son, the entry of the young bride was seen as a competition in the game of social power, control, centrality, marginality and the age. In this game the son was but a helpless spectator, a mute observer and caught between the mother and the wife, most often the son, brother, husband psychologically disengaged and withdrew or fell back to traditional idealistic role of a son. The woman, the new bride, the young wife was not experienced as a person who would enter to bring joy and happiness to the son, rear a family and enlarge the space. She was seen as a usurper, carving out a space in the heart of the son for herself.

In order to understand the dynamics of the In-laws, it is important to explore the social and cultural context and its underlying processes and the vice like grasp of deeply embedded coding of the relationship. In order to understand the dynamics of relationship and issues between a mother-in-law and a dither-in-law, it is important to explore and understand the Indian social dynamics of mother-son relationship. The cultural coding of Indian society is that to a son, mother is a Goddess to be worshipped. The social coding is that she is always good, caring and nurturing and always acts for the good of the son. The coding gets further strengthened by the socialisation process that "mothers can do no wrong". The personal experiences of the mother-son relationships are ignored and held in abeyance and the socialisation processes continues to reinforce the belief that the role of the son is to conform, obey and surrender to the wishes of the mother. Moreover, the feeling and the belief that the mother has sacrificed for the son, nurtured him in the womb, fed him from her own body, lived with the harshness of the husband to protect her son and denied and deprived herself to give the son and many other similar messages get carved in stone and etched for life. Over a period of time i.e., decades and centuries, reinforced by folklore and folktales and the cultural lore of myths and epics, the above coding get deeply embedded in the cultural psyche of the collectively, the social psyche of the family and is finally internalised by the individual. The expectations from the son's behaviour to the mother then get extended and super-imposed to the daughter-in-law.

However, the mother instead of taking role of senior women finds it difficult to do so. She as women lives in the home with the husband as a wife. She has often lived with oppression and compulsions and surrendered her own dreams and wishes in the role of a wife and a mother. As such, at the entry of the young bride and seeing the first flush of her youth and romance the envy, the anxiety of role erosion, the decreasing centrality and significance begin to surface in the relationship. Her wisdom from her experiences and the promises to herself is thrown to the winds. What happens to the relationship of mother-in-law and daughter-in-law? There is a subtle competition and struggle for power to control and possess the son... The mother-in-law competes as the first wife of the house and craves for attention from her son. Basically the insecurities are translated into a very defensive and aggressive behaviour of ruthlessly crushing the blossoming of the bride and creating a space for herself in the home. The dynamics of the relationship is never really examined and the husband / son face immense difficulty and stress. This happens perhaps due to the fact he has never really learnt how to be an adult. Socially a man has never to uproot himself. Whereas the women experiences a dramatic shift in behaviour and role taking as she leaves her home to enter another home and sets of relationships.. The daughter-in-law and mother-in-law syndrome thus replays the psycho-drama of deeply embedded relational coding and interface... If the husband continues to be a son and does not add the role processes of a husband, the cultural and social coding of the mother-in-law and daughter-in-law surface immediately and play havoc in the homes and with each other. The first few years of marriage are the most traumatic in the relationship between a mother-in-law and dither-in-law, and also sister-in-law if she is unmarried. The same processes are repeated for the new bride where she has to encounter the power struggle between the two women – via the mother-in-law and the sister-in-law and her own entry and encounter with the two. For now the new bride is the intruder and the outsider. The whole social dynamics is further made complex when the sisters of the brother are significant and even not so significant in the house.

There are situations, for example, where some husbands wish for and expect from their wives open expressions of affection, social skills to relate to their friends, and participation in social life. The mother-in-law, on the other hand, wants a coy bride who is invisible but always at her beck and call. She needs essentially a traditional, ideal 'bahu' who would be obedient to her. Caught between the two, the woman lives in a state of anxiety and often in fear. She is torn between two conflicting sets of values and her own expectations and dreams. The introjects from her childhood and education, both emotive and cognitive, are also challenged by the experience of being married. Faced with all these, often contradictory pressures, the woman attempts to redefine what she as an individual would like her role and space to be. But she has very few options. When she comes with her own expectations, and joins her husband who is in turn, moving away from the traditional role of being a son, she incurs the wrath of her mother-in-law. Conversely, when she attempts to please and accommodate the mother-in-law, she faces her husband's resentment of being let down. Torn between the two, the woman ends up in a 'no role' situation and has to keep her own expectations in abeyance. (Parikh I,J and Garg, P,K , 1989)

Once the marriage has taken place, the encounter between wife and husband is socially romanticised around all the rituals before and after the marriage. At home when the first event of encounter and conflict between the wife and the in-laws takes place with no support from the husband, it remains as a hurt in a woman. Second episode, third episode, and a process of cumulative negative emotions start building up. The residue of each event or episode overtime acquires monolithical, undifferentiated mass of negative feelings. One more insignificant or significant event and the whole bubble of the past pent-up feelings bursts ,resulting in crisis. This is experienced by each woman as she passes through and lives with the pre-conceived notion of traditional cultural social codings, where the expectation from marriage and the husband is very high. The women visualise entering a fairy-tale world of romance where only love flows, and where one finds the ultimate peace, joy and happiness. Very soon they discover the relational issues and experience entrapment where action freedom may or may not be there. Moreover, they do not experience psychological freedom or space in their new home. What follows is either sacrifice, feelings of rejection, and non-appreciation , and/or a search to create their own space and home. The interface between husband and wife unfortunately never goes beyond looking at each other as husband and wife and never as experiencing each other as a man and a woman and as two different human beings.

There is still a lurking belief in Indian society, Indian organisations as well as with men in the organisations, that women's entry into organisations takes away their attention from social and familial roles. As such, women, men and organisations are pulled and pushed between accepting women's entry into organisations and it simplifications on their multiple social roles. These dilemmas of women, men and organisations have arisen from the fact that the role of women and men were designed in the society anchored in the agrarian society. The new role definitions anchored in the industrialized society with formal work organisations and women's new roles in the society have not fully matured. The socialisation processes and the codings of women's and men's role are deeply embedded and new role definations of women and men are held at the cognitive level. The internalisation of these new role definations as living processes is yet to emerge. Most organisations recruit very few women in managerial positions. At some level organisations want to recruit women but an on another level the organisation's ambivalence comes through as whether women can cope up with their demands, challenges and pressures and whether they will be able to sustain their performance. This ambivalence is reinforced by the choices made by the women during the early years of their career path. Women experience dilemma of choices around whether they wish to continue with the career or respond to the social roles and social systems. In terms of knowledge, capabilities and skills the women who are recruited are of the same calibre as the men. Their performance also conveys commitment and involvement. However, the women also have to make certain choices around marriage and their social roles in homes and families. (Parikh, Indira. J., W.P.No.98-5-02, May, 1998).

Women's Entry Into Work: First Steps to Climbing the Corporate Structure

Women have now been in work organizations for over four decades. They have played a significant and contributing role in the growth, culture and performance of organization. This reality makes it imperative that organizations explore the specific issues which confront women, men, and organizations by women's sustained presence and increasingly taking higher responsibilities, decision making roles and their rise in the corporate ladder.

As women have risen in the corporate ladder they have acquired leadership roles. Women in leadership roles encounter issues of handling power, exercise of authority, providing direction and new choices for organization strategies, participation in policy formulation and strategy implementation, and interface with the external environment. Simultaneously, women encounter the issues of interface with superiors, colleagues and subordinates. The women in their leadership roles are key role-holders both within and outside the systems. Women encounter dilemmas in taking leadership roles. Some of these dilemmas are anchored in the socio-cultural context, the organization culture of external business, environment, as well as in their own maps and definitions of role taking. Often the issues revolve around maintaining boundaries between personal and professional roles and relations, being both efficient and effective in performance, and achievement and managing finally all systems.

Organizations which design career path for women face issues of promotion, appraisal, competition between men and women colleagues, stereotypes about women in leadership roles and positions, and the personality characteristics of women in leadership. Research findings (Parikh I.J 1990, Parikh I.J and Shah. N 1992, Parikh I.J 1998, Parikh I.J and Engineer M.F 1999) suggest that women are capable and competent, are able to take decisions, are autonomous, and do exercise authority. They take significant responsibilities and aspire for positions which are appropriate to the tasks they are doing. More and more women opt for careers or profession, make hard choices, strive for performance and achievements and finally succeed to reach senior and leadership positions. In doing so, women also experience greater stress as they combine work, career, and roles at home, thus generating dynamics of push and pull from work and home settings and personal and professional roles.

Women in Leadership Roles: Organisational Context

Organizations have transformed since their inception through industrialisation. Industrialisation in India is 100 years old. However, the conceptualisation and formalisation of organizations as we know them today is about five decades old. As part of Management Development, programmes for Women and Leadership Roles are designed and conducted at the Indian Institute of Management, Ahmedabad (IIMA). From 1980 till date, programmes on Women in Management are offered to women managers on issues of role and authority. The aim of the programmes is to assess where women are with themselves and the organization in leadership roles. Women have moved from managerial positions to managerial leadership and eventually to leadership roles.

Objectives of the Programmes:

- The programmes aimed at providing a setting where women in senior leadership positions could explore the influence of the organization on their role and environment in which organisations operate.
- The programmes also aimed at providing an opportunity where women managers / leaders could explore their leadership role in organizations as well as discover their life space, in turn to discover wholesome ways of managing personal dreams and career paths.

Profile of Participants and Organisations:

The participants consisted of a cross-section of women managers from India and Srilanka holding positions from Creative Supervisors to Senior lecturers to Dy.Managers in Finance and Marketing to Managers in the field of HR and Marketing, to Asst . general managers in Banks and holding positions of General secretary, Collector and District magistrate in the government. They represented a diverse mix of public sector and private sector companies, banks and financial institutions. Women from organizations like Refineries, Product marketing companies, Automobile, Agriculture, Communications and Media, and Educational institutions or Universities of post graduate systems, also participated.

Methodology:

The programmes was divided into two parts (1) A conceptual module, (2) An experiential module. The conceptual module was discussed in the first part. Participants were provided with an overview of transformations occurring in the environment in organization, in its structure and management practices. Issues of policies and strategies; diversity of tasks and people; issues of authority and leadership; and organization processes which were also undergoing change. The module explored issues of commitment, managerial role, attitudes, excellence in performance, creativity in organization and approaches to problem solving.

The second part focussed on the experiential module where the exploration was around life spaces, processes of socialisation in both family and work settings and crystallisation of women's leadership role and identity. The exploration was around how women could take charge of their life space and systems and give shape and meaning to their own life.

Experiences of Organizational Transformation By Women in Leaderships Roles:

The women shared their lives and experiences of growing up as well as their experiences in the organisation. The observations were:

- Women have entered various new professions which are not traditional like, teaching, nursing etc., Earlier women entered work not out of choice but due to economic reasons or some calamity befalling them and their family.

- Women's entry into formal work organisations has been a decade later then men. Women, like men carried social, cultural and personal maps from their traditional roles to the work places.

- Women are performing dual roles where priority needs to be given to the home-front as it is the women who manage the household. Although many felt that times are changing as increasingly the husband's role is supportive to both women and home. However, women continue to carry feelings of guilt when it comes to their interface with children and anger when it comes to their interface with in-laws. The social-coding and the cultural-coding, eventually becomes a personal coding resulting in dilemmas of marriage around relationships and specially motherhood.

- Women end up taking up more and more responsibilities at work and often work for 16 hours a day. However women take a step backward in taking leadership roles and positions. Not many have broken through the senior management cadre to reach the higher echlons of management.

- Increasingly there is a change of attitude amongst men in perceiving women who are working (Parikh, Indira J, November 1989). Earlier, if a women was successful the assumption was "somebody else e.g a man was behind her success". There was invariably a postulation of a godfather. If a women was friendly with a male colleague – it was always felt that she was having an affair. Platonic relationships were deemed to be improbable. However, many women felt that there is definitely a shift in these perceptions. Today if a women is succeeding it is perceived that she is hardworking and she has earned the position. Women experience a constant pressure to perform and prove themselves in their work place. They face a constant challenge to achieve and prove themselves that they are capable, competent and deserve the promotion and the position.

- The women at work experienced that the women peers were not supportive of women whereas their male counterparts accepted them and were more supportive.

- In a hard core male dominated society, women continue to deal with personal stereotypes and remarks around clothes, dressing and attire. "Silly questions" are asked in interviews which are generally aimed to dissuade women from taking the up the job or push her to guage her resillience or dislocate her from her confidence. Women have learnt to survive and face the reality as a challenge. Women have learnt to deal with such situations logically and rationally or by being nonchalant under these circumstances.

- Women are perceived and related with differently than their male colleagues at the work place. If women present themselves as weak and mild, they are exploited. If they are assertive they are perceived as aggressive.

- The aggressiveness is reflected in women acquiring strong opinions, getting entrenched in arguments, loosing flexibility and negotiability, insensitivity to others opinions and feelings, becoming closed, loosing openness and empathy and overall acquiring an attitude of "I know better" (Parikh Indira .J, WP.no. 98-05-02, 1998).

- Some women shared that at higher levels there are generally men who occupy the significant positions. Women are fewer and far apart. Women experience discrimination in processes leading to promotion. Often the organization policies are different for male and female employees. For eg. in one of the organisation the policy of medical reimbursement for dependents favoured men. Men could claim medical expenses for their parents but a women could not do so for her in-laws or her parents. However, there are changes in the organisation where some women shared that they did not face any such gender bias in their organizational policies.

- Most women believed that there is a shift in mindset of how women are experienced in the organziations. More and more men are accepting that women are competent, intelligent and capable. Women can generate resources. In some profession, women are even considered better than men and in some organizations women are appreciated in terms of being hard working and also in terms of the values and beliefs they carry. The earlier myths which perpetuated in the organization that women's success has a sexual connotation or an impression that women's success is due to a god-father is definitely being replaced by women being regarded as competent, capable, hardworking and committed. Many women felt that though these are the first healthy signs, a large multitude of women still continue to live with stereotype images and expectations of women.

Addressing the issue of **Life Space**, the women brought to the life space, social-cultural codings of being a daughter, wife, daughter-in-law and a mother. Women largely carried guilt around the role of the mother and resentment against the husband for not supporting their initial career aspirations. There were some husbands who were supportive as well as encouraging which made life easier for the women. The complex interplay between Self, Role, Identity and Systems created the juxtaposition of life space of women which had many conflicting nuances of growth and opportunities or surrender of their dreams and apsirations in the name of being good daughters, wives and mothers. The themes which emerged from the discussions of the women reflected the following:

- Although the women accept that they are capable, competent, and committed, they grappled with issues of independence and autonomy. One participant identified a rebelliousness herself and claimed that she did not need to 'ask anyone' before she made her own choices. She did not want to be under any obligation and so directed herself towards a self-contained and self-reliant stance. However, this stance was not conducive to creating, building and fostering relationships.
- However, many grappled with this kind of unresolved coding. The participants had learnt how to balance it but it had resulted in their being overengaged and stretched.

What became clear was that social role codings from the social system and also personal aspirations are impacted by social, cultural and familial codings. Both women and men live with these deeply embedded social and cultural continuities. Continuities give us meanings, anchoring, belongingness, stability, security and code of conduct as we grow up in family settings and as we experience and carry these cumulative experiences. The question confronting women are the kind of departures the women would like to or wish to make. What new beginnings would they make? There are also discontinuities, which we experience as part of changes in the environment which provide new choices and opportunities. If women make departures from social codings, they have to choose to listen to their own voices, choices and actions which they initiate. Unless, women start looking at these issues and deal with deeply embedded social codings of the past, it becomes very difficult for the women to achieve both social and psychological freedom for themselves. Moreover, unless women achieve this freedom they largely carry feelings of guilt which keeps haunting them and inhibits meaningful responses to the roles. They either surrender or rebel. Therefore there is a need to differentiate between action freedom and psychological freedom. Social and psychological freedom gives women many choices and alternatives to redefine and redesign their roles. Social freedom is given when the society transforms itself but the psychological freedom is experienced and acted upon with responsibility and commitment to self, others and the system simultaneously.

Given the above assumptions both of the agrarian and industrial society women's role in today's organizations can be put in the context of their present life space. The key question explored and reflected upon was – to whom does the life space of a woman belong to? Do Women have their own identity? How do they play their roles? How do they take leadership roles? Figure 1, presents the key constituents of women's life space as experienced by them.

Figure 1
Life Space of Women

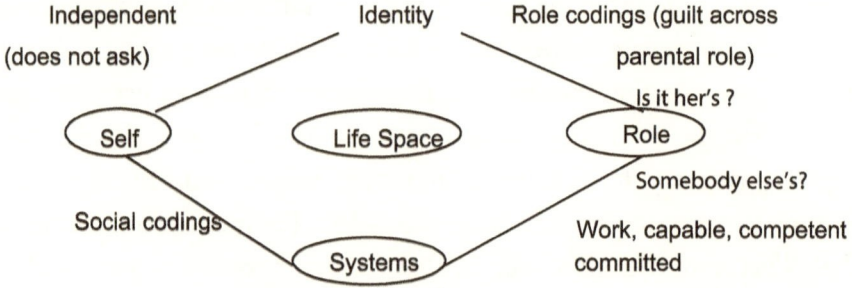

- The 'Self'consists of all that is held within – the emotions, feelings, wishes, dreams and aspirations.
- The 'Identity' of women consists of all the meanings, the multiple roles as they evolve over a period of time, the choices and actions initiated and withheld and the paths chosen consciously or unconsciously.
- The 'Role' refers to the location and space available in the system or not available, the opportunities aspired for and boundaries laid down.

'Systems' reflect a space of belonging. Women grapple with the feeling whether home and work represent their own space, and whether they have ownership of these life-spaces. The perception is that the home space belongs to the father/husband and the work space belongs to male colleagues. They are largely operative in other peoples spaces and as such they have no personal belonging.

There were a few participants from Sri Lanka whose experiences were quite different. However, they did experience a lot of social pressure from their social roles. Moreover, like anywhere else they also experienced a lot of work pressure. Their jobs were very demanding. Their bosses were ruthless in their approach when it came to standards of performance. The pressure from in-laws was also experienced but mostly in those siutations where the in-laws were less educated than the daughter-in-laws. In such situations even the male-counter parts had more demands and were not very understanding. However, women who lived with their parents even after marriage found support in child rearing and freedom from parental anxiety towards their own children. This really freed them to engage with work settings as they did not go through the feelings of guilt and acceptance from the in-laws, and the parents came through as both caring and supportive.

Dilemmas of personal and work life:

The group when exploring and analysing their life spaces, felt that if they divided their life spaces between, work, and other roles, they would get the following distribution in terms of their psychological space as seen in fig. 2:

Figure 2
Life space of a working women vis-à-vis home/family

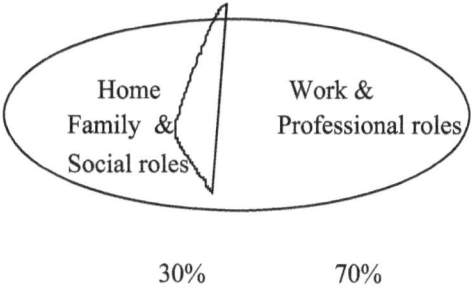

30%   70%

- Work takes about 70% of the women's psychological and physical space and time.
- Home, family and social roles take about 30% of the space and time.

If the women further distributed their time and space , the role of mother demanded the largest psychological and social space as seen in fig. 3:

Figure 3

Distrbution of Social Roles and Spaces

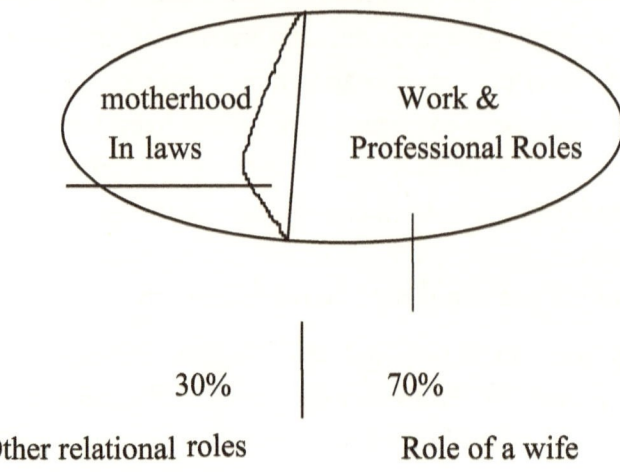

| | 30% | | 70% |
| | Other relational roles | | Role of a wife |

- In the social roles and spaces,
- 80% of the space is for motherhood, 10% of the space is for the in-laws
- 5% of the space is for other related roles, 5% of the remaining space is for the role of a wife.

This dynamics creates immense stress in the husband-wife relationship. Motherhood creates guilt at the deprivation the children voice for the expectations of a full time mother rather than a part time mother. The in-laws largely are not supportive but demanding, complaining and criticising. Moreover, they add to the guilt of motherhood by criticising and evaluating and judging her involvement in work negetively. The children feed on these pulls and pushes and further add to her guilt. Other social roles from the woman's own parental family and the vast network of social relationships make further demands on her space and time. The more she is engaged and enjoys work the more discontent is voiced by the larger extended system.

At the professional level there are relational as well as systemic issues of responsibility, authority and accountability. Issues around travel, work-allocation, performance appraisal, promotions and similar other issues. Women get torn between being a professional and being a homemaker. The explorations and discussions highlighted the fact that for women although their mind worked as a professional, their heart worked as a traditional homemaker. The unfortunate part about the life spaces of women was the fact that while large part of the psychological world of women's life space is utilised in social role-taking, a key issue which rarely gets addressed is the issue of the encounter between man and woman. This is one encounter which has a very new dimension in the formal work settings. Women and men work and relate to each other without the baggage of their social roles.

The question therefore for women to ask themselves is, ' how long were they willing to see themselves get into a mode where they lived for social roles and work roles , and had no life space which they can call their own ?' ' What would be the shared space, which they would create for themselves and with their husbands as an encounter between woman and a man preparing to create a home and a family relevant for the times ?'

Having explored the role and identity issues the women explored the issues around **entry of women into work, stages / phases of work, and interface issues with superiors, colleagues and subordinates .** The group then participated in an open discussion where they discussed about their entry into work, their experiences (both positive and negative) and how they had coped with emerging situations and how they managed in a male oriented work culture, to acquire leadership positions and roles. Some of the personal experiences shared by women reflected the following:

- One of the woman participants joined the organisation at a manager level. Her entry according to her was very smooth.

She did not have much difficulties with male colleagues, except with one or two who reflected social expectations and stereotyped roles as at that time not many women had entered the organisation at the managerial level. There were and are many men even today who have never seen a woman working in a position of power and therefore are not skilled at handling such a role of women. With these mindsets, the participant had to face remarks like " are you interested in such and such a person" or a "comparison with wife" was made. She remarked that many men felt, that the actual place of woman was at home and not work. To handle such mindsets she managed the situations very graciously. She interfaced with male colleagues as far as tasks were concerned, in case of meetings and during travel if flights were delayed when she was travelling with them.

- One of the participant, was in the sales department and was required to do a field job, where she faced a lot of discouragement from her male colleagues dissuading her to leave the job as they thought that she would not be able to do it. There was a lot of pressure experienced and she felt she was under a microscope. Many of her male colleagues and seniors would comment and remark "she won't tough it out"? "Wait and watch". This attitude in fact made her more determined to take the assigned job as a challenge. She worked hard and undertook selling assignments and completed lengths and breadths of the states by merely slogging it out. Wherever she went she had to prove herself. There was no easy acceptance. She took bus journeys with men, sometimes, even at nights which surprised them. They thought that she must have joined sales department due to some financial difficulty otherwise why would and how could a woman do this job? She was rejected for many excellent job offers in the beginning but she would just go ahead re-apply and challenge them by remarking –"you have to see the horse and bet, if you don't its your loss, not mine".

With this confidence and determination she would set aside all barriers. There was performance pressure even from the lowest rung of ladder. She had to face rough language spoken by sales representatives on tour, who would crack dirty jokes taking no cognisance of her presence. She would keep her cool and patience. Finally there came a day when she broke through the barrier and accomplished professional excellence. There were some male colleagues mainly MBA's who had very exploitative mentality and would not hesitate to give open invitations to her to come for late night parties, movies etc and when she refused she was given threats about her appraisal during promotion. She felt as if her job was a kind of "Baptism by fire". One could either swim or sink. The underlying message given to her was "If you want to work like a man, wear your pants and work".

- There were times when a participant had to appraise a male subordinate elder to her. She found it difficult as the male subordinate would remark, "your age and my experience age is the same".

- Many organizations have a culture where to be qualified as an MBA is considered as having an edge above others. For one of the woman participant who was in such a situation it was a constant challenge for her to prove herself, build rapport and credibility for herself through excellence of performance.

- Many women felt that men also have a habit of putting the women colleagues into a slot – like personalising relationships and considering them as their daughter, sister, mother or similar social roles. Instead of a professional relationship they personalise through social relations and social interfaces.

- Another woman who had a field job had to face many insults but that did not discourage her from performing well. Finally her potentials were realised by the authorities who shifted her to a more responsible job. She felt that once men realised the woman's working style, her approach to work, her commitment they accept her, but reluctantly. However, she has to confront a lot of challenges. But once in the leadership role the climb is smoother.

- Another element which most women strongly felt was that the most dangerous and threatful are their female counterparts who get into a mode of gossip, especially with their male bosses if the women colleague is successful and is performing well. Jealousy is tackled by pointing fingers, talking and enlarging minor matters and giving them larger than life shape.

- The Srilankan participants felt that earlier in their organisation there did exist an impression that female members cannot take responsibilities and therefore decision making roles and responsibilities were given only to men. However, they felt that gradually attitudes were changing, and women were empowered to take responsible jobs. Over the years women have proved themselves with their capabilities in the organization.

Future Scenario:

As the world enters the next century and a new millenium, what is the future scenario in both the social and work settings and what are the new spaces to be designed for women?

Some of the themes reflected by many women are discussed below:

- There would be equality in salaries for both men and women. "Equal pay for equal work" would be more and more operative.
- The organizations would work on merit based promotions and not promotions based on gender.
- An attitudinal change which fosters in both women and men a sense of ownership of tasks, commitment to work as teams and, responsibility for organizational performance would emerge.
- A more work based and professional culture in an organization would emerge so that social strereo types would be minimised.

- Men would be educated to accept women at field work and in all spheres of work.

- While recruiting new candidates, rejection of a candidate on the basis of gender would be minimised.

- There could be campaign within the organization to sensitise people on gender friendly organization. Company policy could take care of women's protection in the form of an act which allows punitive action to be taken for the wrong committed. Even personal comments could be discouraged and objected.

- Organizations to become more family sensitive.

- Organizations to provide a gym or stress relieving mechanisms or run classes on meditation / yoga after or before starting work.

- Facilities like crèche, or nursery for small children of women attending office, would generally become the norm.

- Even facilities like a shopping mall within the organization which takes care of vegetables, fruits, medicines and other day to day requirements, which the men/ women can shop ofter office hours, would be provided.

- The flexibility in work hours both for men / women would be given. The choice of completion of task either at home / work place would be given ensuring that deadlines would be met. The focus would be on output or delivery of work rather than quantity of time spent in the work place.

- Women today rise to positions of being functional heads, but very few reach the position of a CEO. Hope was reflected that women would reach the top positions.

- Among the social changes, women are marrying late –(28 years – 30 years), they are even deciding not to have kids, single parenting is an easy option considered by women. Today even many men prefer educated and working wives and take pride in their success. Men are supportive and the trend is changing where they are also prepared to look after kids, by working flexi-hours.

- Many women felt that a workshop of this kind where women issues were focused and dealt with could be undertaken more often as it would empower many other women to come up in their career and it could also be a useful eye-opener for men of this generation.

- The trend is changing. Earlier women seeked for a job. Then they aspired for satisfaction along with job. Later they aspired for recognition. Today some have reached leadership positions in the corporate structure and have proved they can do it.

- The organization's policy to recognise the fact that if men are transferred their wives, and their jobs could also be taken into consideration. Success of men due to transfers need not result in uprootedness of women. There could be a balance. Organization policy could also focus on keeping families together.

- More and more women are reaching higher levels. However, the policies in majority of organizations are made keeping in mind only the men. That could change.

- There could be training programs formulated for men to handle the situation where women is their superior.

- Organizations could have internal counsellors to deal with employee problems.

- In organizations the decision making machinery still vests with men. Women could also be given the opportunity to make decisions as they have better perception and are better lateral thinkers.

- Sharing of work between men / women could take place. Due to social codings of the past, home is still seen as women's space. That could change. More and more men could join the women in managing the internal interface of the home environment:

At an address at the inaugural event in Leadership series, the president of the Penn University shared her experiences on 25th Feb. 1998, excerpts of which are presented below:

- She felt that success should not be measured in terms of polarities. i.e, either as fail or pass. The label-'success' or 'failure' has an impact on self-defination. Self-defination or Self-fulfillment could be sought by cherishing and searching for complexities, embracing ambiguities and risks and rejecting polarities.

- Leadership roles emerge when one follows the heart by doing what they love. Passion and vision are the hallmarks of leadership.

- Women are gifted with the skills that they can develop as professional strengths to become effective leaders. The ability to bring people together to encourage dialogue, build consensus, and share problems and most importantly understand the social and emotional needs of others –all these qualities can bring about a mind-boggling change in the organisation as all these are effective qualities needed to be a leader.

- Competitiveness is a quality essential for great leadership and many women tend to shy away from it. Healthy competition leads to internalised goal-setting and less fear of success. The willingness to share ideas, take risks, acquire new skills, learn new areas and forge new kinds of relationships, having other people know what you think and how you feel , and getting out of shackles of self-doubt can go a long way in creating an environment which stimulates the release of Leadership potential in women.

- She felt that in raising a child, one understands and learns about one's self. The child rearing expands the definations of success and commitment to leadership as it becomes a challenge for the parent to make the world a better place for his young one. It is a challenge for every mother of today's generation to offer to their children, especially a male child , the oppurtunity to see the gender gap closing. The children of tomorrow stand for a generation which is shaped by the changing roles, concerns and problems of women and men, where there is more equality at work and at home. A healthier and happier society will emerge if there is involvement of men in supporting their wives careers and parenting their childreen. It would also help evolve more women in leadership roles.

- Women in Leadership positions will emerge if they follow a mission to value and seek for achievement keeping the humanity, perspective, sense of humor and sense of proportion alive.

Creating new spaces – the work and the home space:
A) Transformation in the concept of work:

Transformation in work and organizations also impact the role of women . As organisations increase the recruitment of women, some will enter the organizations to only become job oriented at work and homely at home. The concept of "minimum amount of time for optimum amount of returns", is emerging. The other set of women will emerge where focus would be on career where home is important but marriage would be a choice. Becoming career-oriented will also give way to the issues of relating with subordinates, colleagues and superiors. In the Indian social reality, a working woman is an immense security and asset for the husband as together they can have a life style which otherwise would not be possible. Organizations and women in organization create space and opportunities for women and men to relate to each other.

Work space is also a space where healthy work relationships get created. In an enduring ongoing social relationships of a husband and wife the partners search for fulfilment of multiple levels of relationships. Sometiems, one cannot find the multiplicity of expectations from one relationship. There are elements of emotional, biological, intellectual and social role related dimensions involved in relationships. Organizations could focus on providing learning opportunities for men and women to relate with each other as human beings. As more and more women are becoming professionally oriented with increased self-esteem, and living by on their own values and beliefs, many of the traditional modes of differentiating home and work will come under review. Both women and men will arrive at mature ways of relating with each other without negating or threatening the social systems and social roles or denying the professional choices of growth.

An element of choice respecting each other's boundaries will emerge. The myths about the professional women as those who have given up femininity and are aggressive will also come under critical review. The work will become an integral part of women's growing up, where she educates herself and which will give her a meaningful dimension in life.

B) Transformation in the concept of home and family:

As more and more women work and grapple with issues of guilt of mother's role, the very nature of home is undergoing change. What is the meaning of home? What is a real home space? And whom does it belong to? These days with fewer children homes are dictated by children and not parents. Does the home belong to individuals/ or is it a shared space? If it is a shared space, then what roles will the mother, father or both play as individuals, what roles will the children play and what roles would each and every member play individually as well as collectively?

Concept of family is changing. From a joint family, the families are breaking up into nuclear family set-ups. Single parenting, week-end marriages, long distance marriages, international marriages, living-in arrangements, and similar new modes of enduring relationship are emerging. Both women, men and the children would have to respond to the expectations and recongfigurations of such relationships and their impact on their lives.

Conclusion:

Women need to ask themselves whether they are aspiring for a job, a career, or a 'higher calling' in life, since leaders are motivated from the inside-out. Their drive comes from within and is exhibited by their outward behaviour. Although a very few women may be priveledged to achieve congruity between the 'calling' and their career, since many economically deprived women are forced to earn their livelihood. Nonetheless, the point is well taken, if one follows one's heart, if one is flying with a tail-wind, propelled forward by inner urge and passion. We believe that counselling / career planning oppurtunities if available to young women at an early age could go along way towards incubating the leaders of tomorrow.

Women are experienced in managing one of the most complex organisations imaginable – the household, with its many human interfaces and interplay between the sexes, different age groups and different stake-holders. Women have learnt over the centuries the art of negotiation and reconciliation and qualities of patience and understanding, along with an inherent quality of emotional intelligence. All these transferable skills can be brought to bear upon the workplace making it the richer, from these valuable experiences.

Perhaps by addressing and answering the two questions below, one can conclude on a positive note about women becoming successful leaders in the next century!

What Leadership Roles will women play in future?

The genesis of the answer lies in careful examination of the question itself! Perhaps in future as true meritocracy becomes manifest, the question itself will be unnecessary since leadership is in no way inherently constrained by 'gender' but only by 'gender-biases'. In the brave new world which we hope the next millenium will usher in, both men and women will play leadership roles in all aspects of life, become total and complete human beings fulfilling different facets of their inner being at home, at the workplace and in the society at large. Artificial fragmentation and divisive labels such as male and female professionals, housewives and working women etc. will melt away making way for a wholistic as well as wholesome approach to living. Only with this fundamental attitudinal shift, can the fullest potential of man and woman be realised leading to channelisation of human energy into productive and positive endeavours.

What concrete steps can the enlightened organisations take to maximise its human resources—both men and women?

An excellent beginning would be to acknowledge the basic biological difference that exists between the genders, viz., women conceive children and therefore need appropriate maternity leaves and arrangements built into their long-term career plan. Surprisingly, organisations do not plan for these basic differences, and do not work with their female employees to evolve common-sense approaches to these issues. Flexible work arrangements that emphasize outcomes and productivity supported by enabling technologies would also help both organisations and employed women to get the best out of each other.

The significant questions women also need to ask themselves are:

- Are women really in charge of their own life spaces? Does the space belong to women?
- Can women say " this space is ours and we can invite others" and can women say "yes and No" to the self as well as others?
- Are the women open to discovering a stranger in themselves?
- Do women own up the uniqueness of their own existence? In other words, do women truly value and respect themselves?
- Can women give shape to their own destiny?

Women in Leadership Role need to answer all these questions.

"One can invite others into their space but should not hand over the oppurtunity of pruning or trimming and shaping themselves to others in a manner that, others shape or make their destiny", is a message one could reflect upon.

After a long psychological journey, some women do arrive at a new threshold beyond the horizon. The woman's soul is tensile and resilient, having journeyed through the endless and arid wastes of social and psychological space. In this process, she has attempted to discover the wholesomeness of the proactive (i.e, anchored in the self) spirit of human existence. Every society and culture has some women who have crossed this threshold and created a space beyond the horizon. These women are the pioneers who add something more to themselves and make life and the process of living a little more wholesome, dignified and gracious than before. Each step on this path requires a pause to reflect deeply on the elements of the past and the present – to shut the door of the past which has been lived out and exhausted itself and to take a step into the unknown. One of the anchors of the space beyond the horizon lies in the freedom to make a choice and to experience the present. To experience the present, women have to free themsevles from the associative universe and the overwhelming symbols of past experiences. This is a necessary step, as the present has one foot in the past and one in the future. The past contains many memoreis – some good, some bad; some happy, some sad; some creative, some destructive; some glowing with radiance, others with hate; some with guilt, and shame, others with pride and achievement; some with the touch of wholesomeness, others with repulsion. These bitter-sweet memories have added up, drop by drop and day by day, to make life a vast panaroma of experiences imbued with the magic, colour, fragrance and enchantment. The other anchor of the present lies in the space beyond the horizon – where instead of hope there is engagement with the world, instead of dreams there is commitment, instead of aspirations there are choices, instead of ideals there are convictions, instead of bestowal and affirmation there is courage . Time and again, the social code of conduct imposed on women and the role-taking processes defined by the cultural lore, prevent the woman from experiencing the stranger in herself which unfolds in each moment. It tames and tempers her being which is otherwise boundless and bursting with energy. Many a women experience terror – at crossing the threshold to a space beyond the horizon, as this space demands that she takes charge of her destiny and her life space around her. These women struggle to take a few steps forward since their vision of their own life propels them to make a choice. They struggle to confront human existence with resilience. They rise time and again from the ashes to respond to their commitments. They reach out to experience their human spirit and the essence of life. Woman after woman has abandoned the choice to make contact with the spirit of human existence within them. They mortgage themselves at various thresholds and rarely cross them to encounter the space beyond the horizon. At each new threshold they encounter the ghosts which haunt the inner space of their lives and return to being echoes and shadows. The confrontation with this threshold and the space beyond the horizon is really an encounter with the inner realities of the self, others and the system. It is a space to own up to the self and to unfold its resources. These psychological resources are designed for new role taking and making choices for action (Parikh, Indira. J., and Garg, Pulink. K., 1989).

The recent role-models do demonstrate women who have tentatively crossed this threshold and are carving a niche for themselves in various fields and are blazing a new path for the future generations. The new Millennium perhaps would witness leaders who would not be identified by their gender but by their capability, their vision and their competence.

The Road Map for Tomorrow

Introduction: Women Executives in Transition

This chapter is an exploration of the 'Woman' within the context of the 'Workplace' and the 'Country', all of which are undergoing fundamental transformation at the dawn of the new millenium. At a macro level, the country with its 5000 years old culture and history is still to come to grips with the modernism of the new century. Ruled by foreign invaders for centuries and by a well-entrenched internal bureaucracy during the past half century, the nation has been searching for an identity, its place in the sun and an international standing commensurate with its vast population and democratic traditions. The sheer complexity of the country, its heterogeneity, the mixes of tradition and modernity have baffled most observers. In the past decade the country has significantly opened up to trade and commerce and to new ideas, to the 'e' revolution and also to woman issues. On the other hand the divide between the privileged and the dispossessed, the rich states and the poor states, the urban woman and the village woman has paradoxically widened. Moreover, inhuman practices such as child labor continue especially in certain States. On the other hand, Indian women with the privileges of education and global exposure have excelled in business, in the arts and in the sciences. However, their less fortunate counterparts struggle in an environment where infanticide, deprivation, slavery and inequality continue as before.

In this complex backdrop, the India of today, let us examine the 'organisation', the ' woman' and the ' woman in the organisation'. The Indian organisation, be it a multinational, an Indian company, a small business, an NGO or an academic institution is a microcosm of the complexities, paradoxes and conflicts that have been detailed earlier for the country at large. The paternalistic traditional organisations and the exploitative small businesses co-exist with Indian companies and MNC s which have global perspectives and the young Turks who are driving the 'e' revolution in India and the world. Given this diversity, complexity and dichotomy, it is hard to describe a generalized work culture for the Indian organisation. However, one can examine trends and changes that are occurring, bringing with them the opportunities and the problems endemic to globalization of the economy. Surely the trend is towards greater meritocracy, transparency, dynamism and technology-driven progress. On the flip side, the human aspect, 'human-centric' development, can potentially suffer. On balance, women can gain from this new environment in terms of open competition and adequate rewards for merit-based performance. However, this can only occur in the context of socioeconomic transformation. Clearly, only a 'Superwoman' can be a full time CEO of a corporation, a mother of several children and a dutiful wife! For women professionals to fully blossom, we have to not only create a level playing field at the workplace, but perhaps more importantly, an equitable context in the home and in the society. In other words, husbands and families who partake of the women's equity in the workplace have to start contributing to household chores and to child rearing. The technological revolution that has swept through the workplace has also to affect the home front and alleviate the inequitable workload on the working woman. We believe that the future holds unprecedented opportunities for women at the workplace due to changing societal attitudes, globalization of the economy and technological advances. However, these opportunities may be tempered by the relative inflexibility of family structures to adapt to new realities.

Attitudinal Changes among Women Executives – The Search for New Directions

Participants in interviews conducted by the authors (chapter 2) were asked to address the issue, "Where are the women of today headed?" The interviewees shared their thoughts and experiences. The authors have attempted to examine the views of the participants in order to distil contemporary trends and concerns. We hope that this will lead to a better understanding of changing attitudes – both at a societal and at an individual level and an exploration of new directions that working women in India are taking.

Education has been a major reason why today's Indian women have made significant progress. Increased job opportunities have become available and women have tried to break the shackles of the past and proved themselves. According to one participant, it is more important to prove to oneself, 'I can do it' than to prove oneself to the external world. This will make women assertive and confident and create role models for younger women to emulate. A marked increase in assertiveness, independence and career focus was noticed in interviewees from the new generation. Many of these women are better qualified than men and have the ability to professionally excel even in erstwhile male dominated organisations. Women know their rights and due to education, work opportunities, and exposure to the media, women have become more open in their thinking. "Self" has increasingly become important for the women of today, according to one of the participants in our survey. Many have adopted a highly individualistic approach to life. Women are ready to meet the demands and challenges of the workplace. This gives them satisfaction, confidence, emotional and financial security and an identity of their own. The authors believe that the new generation of women executives are assertive rather than fatalistic, ambitious rather than contented and are willing to take the risks inherent in leadership positions rather than accepting the *status quo*. We expect this to lead to a correction in the male dominated power equation within Indian organisations.

Sweeping changes are occurring at a societal level where the family is being redefined. Today the role of wife and mother is but one of many roles that a woman chooses. The family is not necessarily the only nucleus for today's woman whose world revolves around multiple nuclei. This paradigm shift has resulted in emotional replenishment being also found at work. Self-growth has become important for many women. The concept of 'I, me and myself' is becoming predominant and some women find relatedness at work more than what they experience with their friends and relatives. There has been a marked increase in the big cities and the larger towns in the number of working couples. This is sometimes driven by the economic need of having a dual income and/or the woman's unwillingness to interrupt her career for personal objectives, especially motherhood. Urban women in particular are choosing nuclear families, late marriages and postponement of childbearing. A small percentage of young couples do not choose to be parents whereas others choose to delay having children. As women become independent, some have started questioning the institution of marriage. They find it 'commitment with no growth' in comparison to the workplace where they find that 'commitment rewards them with success and growth'. Weekend marriages, single parenting and childless marriages are becoming common in metropolitan centres. Women must strive to attain a situation where they can co-hold and balance both roles successfully. The conditioning and upbringing a woman receives in her childhood is crucial in determining her success. The main ingredient being the realisation of the power she has within herself in achieving her dreams. If she feels empowered within herself, it can go a long way in helping her to face any situation.

In view of the above, the family becomes a place where the role of working women becomes more complex than in the past. Difficulties in balancing dual roles can result in guilt and conflict. In our survey, this was especially true of women who had inadequate support systems at home or at work. Guilt is experienced due to neglect of parental duties resulting in grandparents and helpers raising children. Women are undergoing a transition, and have acquired a 'transitory identity' to which they are holding on, together with the 'identity of the past' which they do not want to let go. So on one hand although they find their dreams getting fulfilled, on the other hand the collective psyche of women which they inherit keeps reminding them of their traditional role, which culminates in guilt. Women were torn between the cognitive and the emotive facets of their personality. Today at the macro-level, women have changed, educated themselves, ventured into the professional world successfully. But at the psyche level or the micro level, the belief systems have not changed. When it comes to performing the traditional role, women have still not been able to break the shackles and it cannot be predicted when the change will come. For change to happen at the micro level inner growth and transformation are required. The challenge is for women to become both emotionally and financially independent, find happiness in themselves and not depend on others for their happiness.

On the flip side, today's women in search of individual identity, tend to become self-centred, ruthless, aggressive and rebellious. It would be useful for women to learn the art of being gentle and yet assertive. Moreover, some of the women in organisations tend to ask for special privileges without necessarily qualifying for them. Some women tend to seek emotional satisfaction from organisations and are disinterested in making a contribution to decision making. These attitudes are detrimental to women's interest in organisations. Also, women who have stepped out in the professional world and achieved success tend to look down upon women who have not chosen to work to pursue professional career. Depending on each individual's priorities it may also be rewarding to be a successful homemaker. It is not necessary for women to be exclusively work – driven or home oriented.

Fortunately nature has made women strong. They are compassionate, sympathetic, understanding and caring. They have inborn and inherent qualities such as endurance, patience and responsibility towards work. They are tenacious and can handle pain and suffering better than men. They have the ability to struggle all their lives trying to achieve a balance. Today's progressive world is better allowing women to attain a balance. A number of working women can handle job – related responsibilities and can do well even without family support. Men on the other hand have not had the experience of running a house as well as having a career. Men are less able to manage their life without family support and are emotionally pampered. Women appear to be more focussed and organised than men especially in handling multiple roles. Today's working women need to leverage these inherent strengths and find their feet within the context of the organisation. Their new found assertiveness coupled with structural changes within the organisation and at the societal level will enable them to successfully evolve from their current 'transitory identity' towards a better defined identity that recognises their work as well as their personal life roles.

Transformation in the Socio-Cultural Milieu

Social transformation not only pertains to redefining Motherhood for working women but also to male managers examining their role as fathers and finding synergies between the two roles. Marjosola.I.A., and Lehtinen.J.(1998) have examined the question," How can one get over one's narcissism, partly generated in childhood ?and how can one prevent the problem from being transferred to the next generation ? The focus has been on the impact of parental relations on the childhood of a male manager where his current family life and the father's role has not been recognized. This is probably because private life and parental duties have been seen as separate from professional life. If male managers can recognize their importance as fathers, they may learn something important from their parenthood for their work as leaders. This means valuing social fatherhood in addition to biological fatherhood as part of a man's life, that is, also as a part of a male manager's life." The authors further state that " the image of managers, of fathers and of masculinity are under re-construction. Being a father and learning social fatherhood from it, may strengthen and diversify the gender identity of a male manager. The images and mythology about managers will be challenged on several levels if we begin to look at male managers not only as heroes of the economic society, but at the same time as parents to their children." If one goes back to the traditional beliefs of child rearing, parenting and schooling, one can better understand the male – female dichotomy at the workplace. Parents were used to appreciating independence, aggressiveness and competitive spirit in boys and believed that the qualities of gentleness, submissiveness and service to others were female virtues. This lead to gender stereotypes becoming entrenched. Due to these past reinforcement patterns, boys and the girls carried with them a gender-related map which superimposed upon their behavioral patterns in adulthood (Powell, 1988). According to Brandt .B. and Kvande.E. (1992)," If a male manager takes parental leave and stays at home to take care of his child, this may break the mythology of what it means to be a real man or a real manager. Parental leaves for males are a way of challenging and reconstructing fatherhood and at the same time they may change ideas and stereotypes of masculinity itself."

Clearly, a fair-minded evaluation of the strengths and constraints of both the sexes is required. There is a need for a mutually agreed to workplace paradigm that enables optimal manpower utilization for the organisation as well as individual job satisfaction and fulfillment to both male and female stakeholders in an organisation. The Woman's Liberation Movement that became extremely prominent from the 1960's onwards was a reaction to discriminatory attitudes towards women. Those times are now behind us (although unfortunately not for rural women), and this is an opportune time to break free from the pendulous shifts between oppression and rebellion. We believe that it is possible to evolve a new paradigm with creativity, boldness and the ability to think afresh. Given the monumental technological progress that has been achieved in the Industrial Age during the last century and the present Information Age, it may be possible to progress towards a 'Human Age' where Technology is harnessed for the holistic development of each individual. Following the successful revolution triggered by the Woman's Liberation Movement, the time has come for women to occupy their rightful place in the workplace and in the society. If "the Child is the father of Man", then perhaps "the Girl-child is the mother of Mankind." The challenge is to achieve Liberation in its true sense in one generation of women, which will then become a self-perpetuating phenomenon.

An excellent article " Women and Households in a changing world" (1991), further elaborates on the need for a holistic concept of human development and the need for social transformation. The authors in the article argue that " the most fundamental attribute of the household as the basic living unit is its ability to meet the material and non material needs of its members. Changes in the form of internal or external relationships, which inhibit the household's capacity to do this, must be considered inimical to the goals of social stability and personal well being. Those that enhance the household's capacity and flexibility must be considered beneficial". The article further mentions that " Obsolete stereotypes and attitudes are a major obstacle to the flexibility that facilitates adaptation. Attempts to modify these through socialization and education will only be successful if attitudinal change is encouraged by real options for new behavior. Women's ability to cope and adjust is constrained by their subordinate position in households and society. Measures which enshrine legal and rhetorical recognition of their rights as individuals, and value of their role should be accompanied by practical steps to support and enhance them. Equitably shared domestic responsibilities and equal access to the economic opportunity would strengthen all households of all kinds and reduce their vulnerability in transitional phases". A recent study by Kinnunen .U. and Mauno .S., (1998), examined the prevalence, antecedents and consequences of work-family conflict among employed men and women in Finland.

Using a sample of 501 employees in four organisations, results obtained from the data showed that "family-work conflict was best explained by family domain variables, (e.g., Number of children living at home) for both sexes, and work-family conflict by work domain variables, (e.g., full time job, poor leadership relations) among the women and by high education and high number of children living at home among men. Family–work conflict had negative consequences on family well-being and work-family conflict, in particular on occupational well-being. The findings suggest that improvements in working life are needed to prevent problems in the work-family interface." We are unsure of the relevance of this in the Indian context and this would be an important topic for local study. However, it is worth noting that the trends observed in this study may be indicative of Indian metropolitan cities and that workplace issues need systemic corrections for the benefit of employees of both the sexes.

Participants in interviews conducted by the authors were asked how the society and family were responding to the New Age women who want to balance the demands of home and career. In general, women were respected by their family members, including husband and in-laws and there was no significant opposition to their assuming a dual role as homemakers and working women. In situations where the family assumed an unnecessarily orthodox stand, women asserted themselves and fought for their rights.

Although there is general acceptance of working women within the family and an appreciation of the benefits of dual income, the familial demands on women are unreasonable.

While the current corporate environment is quite supportive of working women the society at large is still patriarchal. This is particularly so in joint families where the woman is expected to be a dutiful wife, mother and daughter-in-law. Some of the participants in our survey reported a feeling of resentment towards the working women on the part of the older generation women in the family (who may have themselves not had the opportunity to pursue a career) and also subtle differential treatment towards the working son versus the new phenomena—the working daughter-in-law. The traditional Indian mindset expects woman to be a dutiful wife and mother, with scant concern for the efforts she has to put in at the workplace. Moreover the definition of duty according to an elder person in a family is usually inconsistent with a working women's concept of being dutiful. This results in familial tension and stress and a further widening of the generation gap evident in extended families which are still quite common in India.

A large majority of men in organisations have non-working spouses. Many of these women are either uneducated or restrained from developing their careers due to familial pressures. The husband working with women colleagues often leads to insecurity for the traditional wife. Many men do not take the responsibility of mentoring or guiding their wives to a path where she gains an identity. For some men to accept a women in office is easy but to see their own wife working is difficult. Most men still feel, "why should my wife work? what is the need for my wife to work since I can run the house comfortably?" Few see the working woman as a person in her own right, giving expression to her individual identity. The need of the hour is an attitudinal change on the part of society, in terms of accepting a woman as she is, and not as they think she should be.

Clearly, this is a transition phase where women who perform the roles of mother as well as working person need to be supported by husbands who also could learn to perform two roles. In a joint family situation increased fair play and sensitivity towards the needs of the working woman are needed. Although working women get a lot of encouragement and support from their husbands, they do not get any domestic or household help from them. The challenge before the women of today is to bring up their male progeny in a manner that they also learn to manage multiple roles right from the formative years. Our research showed that times are rapidly changing during this transition phase and the environment is becoming more liberal and accepting of working women. The prototypical Indian mother-in-law is also changing and cannot be stereotyped. Women have started voicing their feelings. Openness and communication is helping them to build bridges at home with in-laws, hopefully heading towards a brighter and better tomorrow. Women increasingly know what they want, where to reach and are exercising their right, to choose and shape their own destiny. Women have also become more independent due to financial security. In many cases, the husband is now perceived more as a friend who feels proud to see his wife progress in her chosen profession. Although women are capable and efficient at the workplace, the problem arises when they are also expected to play their traditional household role without additional support from the family. We believe that realism should be brought to bear on this situation and that new balances have to emerge within the home and work settings. Changes in the upbringing patterns of children and education will be the drivers of this transformation for future generations.

Education and the Information Revolution as Drivers of Change

The way forward lies in education-centered societal transformation. This is particularly relevant in the Indian context given societal disparities, social taboos, widespread illiteracy and the pre-dominance of rural women. Dr.Mashelkar, R.A., (Director General,Council for Scientific and Industrial Research) in a Presidential address in the 87th Science Congress meet held at Pune on January 3, 2000 proposed a five-point agenda focussing on child-centered education where the role of teachers and schools is stressed as being important in molding the children of tomorrow. On one hand we have the technological revolution, but on the other hand our systems of education are archaic. The Indian child instead of being molded by " discovery and experience ", is being taught by " rote and repetition ". The inherent creativity in the child therefore stands diminished. Individuality and imagination are inadequately nurtured in our current education system. India's hallowed tradition of *"Guru-Shishya parampara"* has been significantly compromised in recent

years. Many Western societies today have become centers of learning
due to their respect for Education, and even more so for Educators, who
by definition are not only educated but educate others. Indian society
today has degenerated to the point where criminals win elections from
prisons, corrupt businessmen are revered and gangsters rule the roost.
India, the ancient seat of learning for the world, today witnesses frantic
cues of youngsters outside the U.S embassy to flee the country for a
better education and a merit-based environment. The Indian teachers
of today, underpaid and undervalued are also contributing to the self-
fulfilling prophecy that is our deteriorating educational system.

We would like to submit that it is not the teachers who are at fault,
they are after all a by-product of the society and its value-system. The
mother, the child, the father and the teachers make up this system and
are in turn shaped by the system. Perhaps the best way to break this
negative cycle is to create a new generation of "teacher leaders" with
strong values and a mission to shape the generation of tomorrow. We
quote excerpts from a speech by Mrs. Anu Agha (Chairperson, Thermax
Ltd) at the Eklavya Excellent Award function held on Sept 5, 1999 in
Ahmedabad. According to her, "Teaching is a human activity. Intellect
does not teach intellect. People teach people. No matter how factually
accurate and time-tested our data, true learning emerges only when we
honor the human factor. If we can emotionally reach out to every child
–their interest in learning will be created. The teacher's job is not to
separate the gifted from the ordinary, but to find gifts in the ordinary.
The worth of a student is far beyond academic brilliance. Most schools
take an easier option and have strict entrance exams before they select a
student, and later weed out poor performers rather than concentrating on
upgrading skills of the teachers. Teachers must believe in the unlimited
potential of every student. Potential is invisible to the superficial gaze.
It takes patience and faith to discern it. Each student is a material for a
work of art and a beautiful piece can be sculpted out. On the other hand,
if the teacher does not believe in the student's potential, it sows seeds
of doubt in the student's mind. Picking up negative signals, students

withdraw and stop taking risks. When this happens everyone loses. Teachers must have the humility that there is a lot that they know and that they need to be continuously in search of knowledge and remain student themselves. They also have to realize that there are many things that they can learn from a child. Education needs to move away from teacher-centered learning to a student -centered approach. In teacher-centered learning, the teacher is the expert and the students are sponges that passively absorb whatever is doled out. To make education student-centered would require a lot of creative preparation by the teachers and a high degree of emotional involvement with the students."

In today's Information Age, a child's impressionable mind is significantly influenced by the media. The messages conveyed by the omnipresent TV serials often reinforce gender stereotypes. Although today's Television takes cognizance of the working woman, the role stance typically adopted by female characters is reactionary. Even though such role profiles are not entirely inaccurate, children receive stereotyped messages of woman. For e.g., the mother being portrayed as a submissive housewife or at the other extreme as a ruthless, career-oriented go-getter who ignores her family. A wholesome depiction of a person, male or female, is infrequently found in present day media which seems to thrive on a diet of stereotyped stories and jingles. These coding derived from the institutions of family and school and also from the media are inevitably carried into the workplace by both men and women employees (Powell 1988). This baggage of the past usually comes in the way of creativity, originality and effectiveness at the work place. Thus, the negative energies that are expended at the workplace in re-creating role plays based on these stereotypical coding of the past need to be re-channeled into creative actions and fresh thinking.

Redefining the Workplace: Responsibilities for Creating a New Tomorrow

We have examined in this chapter, 'a road less traveled'. Women across three generations have come a long way in terms of gaining freedom of expression and action which was always rightfully theirs.

The past few decades have also witnessed various experiments in terms of working women balancing their professional and personal dreams and responsibilities. In both men and women, there has been change and transformation, sometimes through pro-active processes and sometimes through traumatic conflict situations. New paradigms have evolved at the workplace, many of which are creative and flexible rather than being rooted in past dogmas. Mattel Inc. has for the first time positioned Barbie doll as a working woman, who carries a brief case and works at a computer terminal in her private office. The working version of Barbie also comes with a gold credit card of her own depicting that Mattel's Barbie is no longer just a pretty face, (Business Week, 1985).

Participants in our survey were asked," how are organisations responding to entry of more and more women at the workplace?" It is observed that men are increasingly accepting of women in the more enlightened organisations. In some cases female bosses have also found acceptance, although such situations are still the exception rather than a norm. It is now possible in some cases for women to surpass their male colleagues at the workplace. HRD departments are increasingly learning to leverage the inborn talents of their female employees in terms of inter-personal skills, crisis management and overall ability to manage diverse roles. The better women managers have an enormous capacity to cope with conflicts and can be more resilient and strong than their male counterparts. Organisations have realized that women are capable, have tremendous capacity to work hard, are sincere, and can be outstanding managers and leaders.

However, some of the women participants in our survey expressed a contrary view. Women managers have negative experiences due to male insecurity and apprehension about women taking over their dominant roles in the organisation. This insecurity is sometimes manifest in wild accusations about successful women. This absurd thinking and behavior stems from an inferiority complex found in certain male managers. Moreover, many organisations are obsessed with short term work goals and financial imperatives to the detriment of human development.

Money seems to be the main currency in the organization, for the employee, for client relationships and for virtually every other work context. This is akin to a pendulum at one extreme which needs to come back to balance in the center, where value building will need much more energy and attention.

Clearly, in today's organisations, facilitating policies and practices for both men and women at the workplace need to be implemented in a manner that is fair and equitable but at the same time productive and efficient. Company run crèches, flexitime, 'e'-enabled work in the organisation and at home, paternity leave etc., are examples of policies practised by progressive organisations. Organisations need to become increasingly sensitive towards personal and familial responsibilities of their female employees. There could also be job-sharing arrangements between two or more women within the organisation. Clearly, adjustments and sacrifices are required from both the organisation and the individual.

The 21st century holds great hope and promise for women in the workplace. The various changes and attitudinal changes that have occurred during the last 50 years bear testimony to the rapid evolution in societal attitudes towards women in general and towards working women in particular. The relatively recent Western way of life, involving dual income families and gender equality has spread throughout the world. It is quite possible that the eras of Technology and Information will evolve into a new era of holistic human development and progress. De-construction of age old patterns, systems and mindsets are leading to a new renaissance in human thinking, gender relationships and synergism across various facets of human life.

Is all the above a wishful thinking? On the one hand we have progressive organisations in India and across the world where men and women both have made great progress. On the other hand, the 21st century still witnesses the hangover of the darker side of the previous century. Gender bias, race bias, age bias continue unabated. It should also be said that women have contributed in equal measure by perpetuating traditional gender biases and often taking self-centred stands when they reach positions of authority. The results and analysis of a survey on working women in the West is found in a book edited by Konek, C.W.,etal (1994). It was found that most career women advocate working harder and better on an individual basis before advocating collective policy or legal changes. They rely on their ability to overcome the odds even if they are built into the system in which they live and work. They are focussed on individual success. The authors in this book opine that although this belief may reflect the participant's optimism and initiative, it may also interfere with their dedication to fight for justice for other women. The authors further suggest that " If we do not work to change a system that includes structural inequities, every women who follows us including our daughters, would start over alone. If we do not work to make our professions, organisations and society responsive to the needs of women, we may unwittingly complicit with a system that underestimates women's worth and undervalues women's work." According to the authors, "The lessons of the past tell us that reluctance to work for structural change may cause a woman to underestimate the willingness of her colleagues, male and female, to engage in partnership strategies for the realisation of social justice and she may underestimate her capacity to influence the transformation of society. By recognising the importance of taking collective action with other women, she may more fully realise her own potential.

Moreover, the progress achieved by women in the workplace in the last few decades does not cut across the board. With vast disparities between women in different countries, between urban and rural women and women in different socio-economic strata, these discrepancies are particularly pronounced in the Indian context. Clearly, a long and difficult road lies ahead. However, one can take satisfaction from the fact that at least the path seems to be in the right direction. Learning, communication and transformation is also likely to be much faster in the new age due to the Internet revolution. Undoubtedly, women have made enormous progress in recent years and hopefully this is a harbinger of overall societal transformation. The progress that has been made needs to be built upon. The new paths that have been traversed need to be reinforced, so that more can travel more easily. Various role-models in India and across country in varied walks of life are now available for inspirational support.

Success Strategies for the Corporate Women of Tomorrow

Research conducted by these authors including surveys of working women in India, indicates that today's women can do a lot more to shape their future. In this chapter, we have examined opportunities and challenges facing women at the workplace, at home and at the societal level. It is necessary for women to more fully understand the environment, exploit available opportunities and become change agents in order to create a better tomorrow for the next generation of working women. A deeper understanding of the environment will better enable women to introspect, determine their own career path and prioritize what is important to them. Although commonalties exist across the spectrum of working women in India, each individual needs to determine her own priorities and then strategize and endeavor to shape her own unique destiny.

Discussed below are some success strategies for working women of tomorrow. Some of these pertain to attitudinal changes and personal transformation, whereas others are practical, action oriented strategies and tactics.

- Women should become change agents and strive for leadership roles within the organizational context. They should avoid taking the path of least resistance and have the courage of conviction to break barriers that come in the way of women assuming leadership roles. Rather than compete, they should lead. Rather than becoming clones of men at the work place, they should leverage their inherent strengths in order to bring new dimensions and value to the organisation.

Women possess the qualities of resilience, patience, empathy, compassion, emotional intelligence, service orientation and an understanding of human interfaces which are arguably superior to many men. These qualities along with business skill sets that education have provided, can be a winning combination that can catapult women to leadership positions within Indian organisations. Women should not loose touch of their femininity but rather bring bear their unique qualities to the workplace. They can bring about qualitative change in the world of business and commerce through their values and by introducing a holistic human development perspective at the workplace.

- Many working women are aggressive but not assertive. This leads to a reactionary negative cycle at the workplace. Women need to be gentle yet assertive in terms of getting across their view point at the workplace. They need to evolve from a reactionary mindset to a pro-active and positive attitudinal frame of mind. They should build negotiability with male colleagues at the workplace, at the same time women need to retain their individuality and personality rather than try to be "someone else" to gain acceptability from the traditional system. Although difficult in the short term, this stance will result in respect for women within the organisation in the long run and a better acceptance of their unique identity. Tomorrow's woman will "listen to her heart beat" since otherwise she will soon become a rebel without a cause.

- It is important for women who succeed in the corporate world to give something back in return for the individual success they have achieved. These women can become successful role models for younger aspirants and can use the power and respect that they command within the organisation to bring about structural changes beneficial to other working women.

- Women need to re-look at their attitudes and roles within the context of the family and home. They need to explore the shared space shared space which they can create for themselves and their husband. This is essentially an encounter between a woman and a man who are co-creating a home and a family relevant to the times. The ability to communicate and negotiate will be important for achieving a harmonious and balanced life. In this context, the husband becomes a friend and a co-traveler on the path of life. Tomorrow's women need to introspect, establish priorities and thoughtfully determine their own life path. Stereotyped definitions of the past are melting away to reveal new choices for tomorrow's woman. For example, should she marry or be a single career person? If she chooses to marry, when should she marry and when should she plan a family? Should she choose a nuclear family or a joint family, either with her husband's folks or her own folks? Tomorrow's choices will be made based on a combination of personal preferences and outside realities, but less so through pre-conceived notions of the past. There is no one right choice. Different individuals will choose differently to suit their own personalities and needs. The only common aspect is the right to choose. Once the foundation of dialogue and choice is established, decisions regarding balancing work and other life roles become easy. Taking responsibility for one's own life is not easy, but is undoubtedly the best option for women of tomorrow.

- The definition of 'home maker' needs to be re-defined to include both the wife and the husband. It needs to be understood by the husband and the family that a free and fulfilled women will be the mother of a strong and free new generation. Families that partake of a working woman's equity need to reciprocate by sharing the woman's workload at home. For the current transition phase to be successful it is necessary that there is attitudinal transformation not just at the workplace but also at the familial and societal levels. We believe that communication, negotiation and assertiveness are important for tomorrow's women to achieve the objectives detailed above.

- Tomorrow's women should see themselves within the context of the age they live in. The Information Age will allow them to leverage available technology to the fullest and to overcome perceived handicaps of the past. Enabling technologies allow the possibility for women to excel in a virtual environment where home-offices, flexi-time etc., become possible.

- Organisations need to more fully understand and realize the latent potential in their female workforce. Policies and systems that are customized and tailored to enable and empower working women can become a competitive business advantage for enlightened organisations. These changes will occur at the workplace only if working women actively seek to be change agents and if women leaders of today look beyond their individual success to bring about structural change for the larger good.

- Women also need to become change agents at the societal level recognizing the power of Education, Media and representation at the political level to shape societal behavior. It is also important for women to fully appreciate the power of education and to realize that it is education that has brought them to the present stage of progress. Sadly, Indian women often under utilize their education and frequently fail to upgrade their professional skill sets after marriage. Tomorrow's women need to focus on continuous education and also on the fullest utilization of their knowledge and skills at the workplace. It is important to understand that the woman is also the mother of tomorrow's generation and her upbringing of children can play a fundamental role in creating a superior new generation of men and women.

Road Ahead

Women managers and women in leadership roles are today a reality. The momentum will continue and the chains will break and the shackles will fall. The glass ceiling will shatter and the women will bring a tempering of the masculine organization structure with gentler and softer human processes . However, this does not mean that compromises would be made on setting standards of excellence or achieving tough mileposts for results. What will happen is that men will take on more challenges and women will walk side by side to respond to challenges. Men will test their endurance by over engagement in achieving targets and women will ensure that a balance is kept and wholesomeness of life space is retained. Time will come to pass when women will bring creativity and innovativeness and men will join to make it a reality. It is the rhythm of the two polarities that a new order organization would be created. Work will pull the best resource and not the gender specific response or gender stereotypical response.

Essentially, society, family, organization and the external environment impacted and pulled and pushed by the media would create spaces for changes and guilt free resolution of dilemmas. In all of this the women need to let go the part of the baggage and shed the externally induced guilt of social roles. They need to listen to the inner voice of silence and fortitude and discover new paths. They need to walk to and discover new directions and accept their own substantiveness and value themselves. It is in this process that the world order will change and transform the existing skewed world order and create a new rhythm.

Women are working in this multifaceted world. The organization scenario changes like a kaleidoscope with every responsibility, accountability and multiple pulls and pushes, which women have faced and came out with success.

In the new order, women will put down roots of a family and discover the freedom of sailing in the open seas. The women will visualize a new horizon and identify directions and make tough decisions. In the cacophony of sounds echoing of the past the women will cross the threshold to listen to their own voices. The silence of centuries will find the first voice, which will beckon women to sail into the unknown and unchartered land to lay the foundations of their growth to contribute to a partnership.

In summary, we believe that successful strategies for tomorrow's working women need to be within the larger framework of the society as a whole. Women need to take responsibility for their own lives and also for bringing about societal transformation.